Talking About God in the 21st Century Marketplace

Talking About God in the 21st Century Marketplace

Debate, Silence or Gentle Persuasion?
Presenting Jesus Christ at Work

A 10-PART STUDY BY
Randy Kilgore

Applying Faith to Work
Marketplace Network, Inc. / Resources for Christians in the Marketplace

The Marketplace Network was founded in Boston in 1993 by the late Dan Smick with the goal of becoming a grassroots movement of career minded people to learn how to serve Jesus Christ as the Lord of the Marketplace. Since its inception, thousands have been helped in their struggle with applying faith to work.

Contact us:
Marketplace Network, Inc.
One Park Street
Boston, MA 02108
tel: 617-227-4226
email: info@marketplace-network.org
web: www.marketplace-network.org

Talking About God in the 21st Century Marketplace
Written by Randy Kilgore
Copyright © 2003 Marketplace Network, Inc.
All rights reserved. No part of this publication may be reproduced in any form without written permission from Marketplace Network, Inc.

ISBN 1-931811-09-1
Published by Marketplace Network, Inc.,
One Park Street, Boston, MA 02108

Scripture quotations taken from the New American Standard Bible®, Copyright © 1960, 1962, 1963, 1968, 1971, 1972, 1973, 1975, 1977, 1995 by The Lockman Foundation. Used by permission.

Designed by DFS Creative Services
Printed in the USA

Table of Contents

Acknowledgements 7
Introduction 9

1   ***Why Bother?*** 11
    COMPANION STUDY:
    Following Philip—Going Where We're Led 89

2   ***Do I Have to Talk?*** 17
    COMPANION STUDY:
    No Longer "Not Yet" 95

3   ***The Gentle Art of Persuasion*** 23
    COMPANION STUDY:
    Breaking Down the Walls Gently 99

4   ***Learning the Importance of Silence*** 34
    COMPANION STUDY:
    When We Shouldn't Speak 105

5   ***What Must Be Understood, What Must Be Said*** 39
    COMPANION STUDY:
    Knowing What to Say 108

6   ***Ready to Give an Answer*** 50
    COMPANION STUDY:
    Showing Ourselves Approved 113

7   ***…Not Forgetting to Pray*** 59
    COMPANION STUDY:
    The Preparation of Prayer 117

8   ***Responsible Workers*** 65
    COMPANION STUDY:
    Responsible Workplace Evangelism 121

9   ***Come, Let Us Reason Together*** 75
    COMPANION STUDY:
    Scripture Is Truth 125

10   ***What If They Say Yes?!*** 81
    COMPANION STUDY:
    Steps of Discipleship 130

Acknowledgements

The author and Marketplace Network, Inc., want to acknowledge the contributions of many toward the release of this book. We appreciate the editing and design work of Derk Smid, whose efforts help the text come alive to the reader. We also want to recognize the tenacious work of an editorial committee who reviewed the document meticulously, adding their insights and direction to strengthen the book and its objective: Ray Bandi, Diana Bennett, Jim Bruce, Chris Chiambalero, Kent Kusel and Susan Smick.

We also wish to acknowledge the support of the Millennium Committee of Park Street Church, whose ability to capture the vision of the marketplace as a mission field encouraged us to press forward with this book. Their financial support in the form of a special grant, added to the generous contributions of Marketplace Network's regular donors, makes this book available to working men and women.

This book is dedicated to the many faithful workplace Christians who carry the banner of Christ every single day.

About the Author

Randy Kilgore brings twenty years of workplace experience to his writing, most of which was spent as a senior human resource manager in the construction and health care industries. He holds a Master of Divinity from Gordon-Conwell Theological Seminary, and undergraduate degrees in both business administration and political science. He and his wife, Cheryl, and their two children reside in Hamilton, Massachusetts. Randy serves as senior writer at Marketplace Network.

Introduction

"Faith is a private matter."

With those five words America's business culture sentences many working Christians to lives of immense frustration. Wrestling with how to do business in a pluralistic society, most companies take the easy route: Making faith taboo on the job. This means the very truth which guides the steps of a believer's life is unwelcome in the place where they spend most of their waking hours.

"Faith is a spiritual action."

With those five words America's church culture sentences many working Christians to lives of immense frustration. Wrestling with how to remain relevant in a culture that seeks to marginalize God, the Church turns inward, leaving the impression that only overtly spiritual acts form true worship of God.

In American society, many people spend more of their waking hours at their jobs than in any other activity. While that may or may not be a positive commentary on our culture, it's a fact that must be considered by churches or ministries seeking to equip Christians to live out faithful lives. Yet, in our work cultures today, most of us have been trained to separate our faith from our work lives. The chasm between the two worlds gnaws at our being, signaling our souls that something is amiss. This comes at a time when the single most common demographic among people in the church is work, and at a time when the culture of that workplace is most foreign to our faith.

This book aims not only to smash the myths that separate work and faith. It also seeks to offer ideas, encouragement and direction for talking about the most important thing in our lives in the place where we spend most of our days—our jobs.

Readers who enjoy exploring Scripture (a practice we heartily endorse!) will want to use this as a Bible study guide in a group or individual setting. To serve that audience, we've developed ten Bible studies and included them to the back of the book. These "companion studies" tie in to the ten chapters of the book, offering individuals and groups the opportunity to discover not only the content of the chapters, but new insights from their own prayer and study.

Others may prefer to tackle the text first, then explore the Bible studies at the end of the book to reinforce the information, and to renew their confidence in the Bible's relevance in today's workplace.

Anyone wishing to reach the hearts and minds in today's biggest mission field, the workplace, must acknowledge the unique role working followers of Christ play in taking their faith into this culture—a culture which has all but forgotten Jesus Christ and seeks to marginalize God. Now more than ever, there is an urgent need for the Gospel to be carried into daily life. What better place could there possibly be to reach seekers for Christ? Do we wait for them to come into our church buildings? Many never will. Do we wait for them to seek out a pastor? Many don't know one. Now more than ever do the "indigenous believers"—those Christians already in the mission fields of accounting, construction and any other honorable vocation—need to be equipped to share their faith with those around them.

CHAPTER 1

Why Bother?

Among workplace Christians, few topics create more angst than discussions around talking about their faith at work. Some of us find the matter offensive, conjuring up images of water-cooler evangelists passing out tracts and pouncing on unsuspecting passersby. Others among us find it frightening, worried that we'll say the wrong thing or that it will adversely affect how our co-workers view us. Most of us simply don't see how we could do it, and don't know where to look to learn how.

Why is it necessary? With the presence of so many churches, with radio and television programs on faith, with evangelistic ministries like Billy Graham's, aren't there ample opportunities for people to hear the Gospel? The answer, frankly, is no!

In nearly all those vital venues, people make an active choice to place themselves where they can hear the message. They choose to go to church or a Billy Graham gathering. They choose to tune into a Christian radio or television station. Even those ministries that reach outside their circle to draw others into them seldom have the marketplace setting as their target. Yet for many in our culture their job defines the context of their life. This means the language they speak is a work language, not a faith language. When outreach efforts garner their attention, those efforts often speak in terms and context difficult for a worker to comprehend.

Just as Adoniram Judson needed to translate the Bible for nineteenth century Burma nationals, so too must those of us familiar with both faith language and work language "translate" God's word into descriptions understandable to people in our work cultures.

That still answers only part of the question: Can't God get who He wants in the Kingdom without us? Yes, He can, but He chooses to work through us. Why is sharing our faith so important? Let's examine five reasons:

1. Scripture commands us to do so.
2. Hell exists.
3. People looking for God are being offered false substitutes.
4. Sharing our faith strengthens our faith.
5. Our faith impacts the practical aspects of life just as powerfully as it impacts our place in eternity.

Scripture commands us to share our faith

Let's be painfully blunt here. The question is not "Do I share my faith, or don't I?" It is "Will I be obedient to the commands of Christ, or won't I?"

Throughout Christ's earthly ministry He rarely encouraged people to tell others about Him. In fact, there is a puzzling frequency to the number of times He discourages people from doing so. Some writers suggest this means we shouldn't feel an urgency to share our faith. They're wrong!

"Not yet" is the theme of Christ's time on earth, not "don't tell." Jesus knew He would not be fully understood without the context of the Cross and Resurrection. It was after these events, when His disciples *could* fully understand, that Jesus issued His Great Commission in Matthew 28:19-20.

In a later chapter we address this point more fully, but here we assert an important truth: The story of Jesus cannot be told without the Cross and Resurrection. Indeed, without those two events Christ might merely be another mystical wise man.

We live in the post-Resurrection era. Everything we need to understand our redemption is available now for us to know. "Not yet" is replaced in our era by "go and teach." Either we do, and are obedient, or we do not, and are disobedient. *How* we talk about God may differ, but *that we must* tell about Him is a certainty.

Hell exists

When my children were small they played a variation of hide-and-seek. Rather than hiding, they simply stayed in plain sight and covered their eyes. Their minds reasoned that if they couldn't see me, I couldn't see them. Our culture plays the same game with eternity: If they refuse to believe it exists, then it must not exist. In a heightened travesty to the lost, even some pastors and theologians have joined the game, denying the existence of Hell!

Even those of us who believe in the existence of Hell dance merrily through life rarely pondering its consequences for our unreached co-workers. Our silence rubber-stamps the hear-no-evil-see-no-evil game the culture is playing.

[Passages dealing with Hell: Matthew 25:41-46; Matthew 8:12; Matthew 5:29-30; 2 Thessalonians 1:9; Rev. 19:20]

Those who fail to respond to the call of Christ on their lives will pay a terrible eternal consequence. Our love for them demands we earnestly seek ways to help them know Christ.

False prophets—people looking for God are being offered false substitutes

The hunger of the soul is a universal truth. Unfortunately, false prophets can temporarily assuage the hunger pangs. These may be as overt as drugs, sex and alcohol, or as subtle as Buddhism, good works and New Age techniques. Jesus said no one would come to the Father except through Him (John 14:6), and that means no amount of noble acts or good deeds buys a pass to heaven (Matthew 16:23).

Not one of these false prophets is timid about making its appearance in the workplace. Cults and pseudo-religions gain greater access through groundbreaking ethical works and health-wealth tomes. Even Christian writers dive into the fray with works on positive thinking and be-faithful-and-be-successful inaccuracies. (See the sidebar *Dangerous Detours* at the end of this chapter.)

Those who have experienced the impact of Christ's forgiveness in their lives are the only ones who know a true satisfying of this hunger of the soul. Either we believe that or we don't. If we believe it, then we must share it with others. If we *don't* believe it, then we are not Christians but rather deists (those who believe in God but not the exclusive claims of Jesus Christ). In that case, we cannot share what we do not know.

We should be troubled by how easily others are dissuaded from continuing their search for answers, and we should want to place Christ on their "menu of available selections" as they begin their search.

Sharing our faith strengthens our faith

Sunday school teachers (and probably every other kind of teacher) often discuss how much they learn while teaching. The act of sharing our faith guarantees it a primary spot on our radar screen and serves not only to help us grow, but to influence all the other actions of the day.

Hearing ourselves say aloud what Christ has done for us (our testimony) and what He means to us (our witness) keeps both fresh in our minds. It also becomes part of our "public face." This changes not only how others behave around us, but also how we behave around others, now that we know they comprehend what we claim.

Our faith can affect our culture

Christians are not called to be concerned merely about eternity. Just as Christ influences our lives, so too does He influence His Creation. God's laws as recorded in Scripture are not mere hoops for us to jump through; they are guides to a more effective experience of His Creation.

Put simply, introducing Jesus Christ into your workplace will change your workplace. That is as true for the receptionist as it is for the CEO.

From the obscure corner of the Roman Empire emerged our heritage of faith, and nothing so changed the history of the earth as Christianity. It is not our efforts that evoke this change, but rather the work of the Spirit in us. While on our own we can't change our workplace, Jesus Christ can and does. That He waits for us to declare Him is a continuing mystery; that He blesses that declaration is an eternal truth.

Jesus Christ changes lives, and changed lives change cultures. We must share our faith when we desire to see those lives changed, and we may then marvel at how it changes cultures.

IN OTHER WORDS...

Dangerous Detours

Visit any bookstore today, and you're almost certain to be bombarded with titles in two categories: business books on strategies for success and self-help books.

For Christians the titles present minefields which should often be avoided. While some of those books contain solid strategies and can indeed lead to success, far too often the objective behind those strategies violates the principles of Kingdom service.

So how do we determine which books are valuable and which ones are not? First, examine the basic premise of the work: Is the focus on personal success? If yes, then warning bells should be going off in our heads. Personal success is not wrong in and of itself, but when that's the ultimate goal rather than a means of improving our ability to do the work God calls us to, then our life is out of balance already. A focus on the latter—improving our service—can make those works on personal success useful to us, but only if we're paying close attention to the seductive influence of shifting our attention to serving ourselves.

Second, any work which offers short-cuts through the truths of Scripture should be dismissed out of hand. That may seem unnecessary to point out. But there are many works on positive thinking, on "unleashing the power within", on visualization and meditation which sound good on the surface but which place humans at the center of the universe, and not God. New Age works, even those containing moderate amounts of wisdom, are especially designed to chart a course to a worship of self, and therefore necessarily away from God.

Third, the spiritual beliefs of the author should be considered. Since we believe that faith permeates all of life, then the writings of those who are not Christians, or who belong to faiths which distort the Bible, consequently are affected by their beliefs. It is wise, therefore, to not only study the basic premise of a book but the author's worldview as well.

Even among Christian books, "success" and "self-help" titles dominate store shelves. These books can be dangerous detours for working believers to take. For example, any book which suggests that obedience and faithfulness guarantee success (a) is not dealing in reality and (b) is very hurtful to those Christians whom God calls on to sacrifice in His service. Success anywhere in life may be a blessing from God, but it is never guaranteed, and no book which makes such a claim should have a place on our shelves.

Finally, there is no substitute in a Christian's life for the Bible. While human writing has its place in our library, every one of those works must be measured against the absolute truth of Scripture. Our failure to assimilate the Bible into our lives makes us ill-equipped to correctly judge the value of other writings, and can lead to dangerous detours.

CHAPTER 2

Do I Have to Talk?

Saint Francis of Assisi is credited with saying, "Preach the Gospel always, and, if necessary, use words." Many Christians latch on to this expression and attach almost biblical status to it. More often than not, they're doing so because they don't want to feel obligated to give verbal assent of their faith.

In chapter one of this book, however, we contend that sharing our faith is a command. Here we want to demonstrate that *verbal* assent is a part of that command. Consider these observations:

1. Even when Jesus told men and women not to tell, they couldn't help themselves.
2. Jesus emphasized its importance when He declared that He would deny before the Father anyone who denied Him before men.
3. What we say reveals our heart.
4. Scripture commands us to give verbal testimony.

"... the stones will cry out" (LUKE 19:40)

It's perfectly natural for us to be nervous about how we tell others about our faith. It is *not* natural if we don't *want* to do so. In fact, if we have no interest in telling others about Jesus Christ and what He's done for us, it may be time for us to check our relationship with Him.

A bold statement? Not really.

Study the responses of those who encountered Christ and a familiar pattern emerges: They marvel and proclaim! The shepherds see the Child and declare the marvel of His birth (Luke 2:8-20). Simeon sees the Baby in the temple (Luke 2:25-32), as does Anna the prophetess (Luke 2:36-38), and both declare Him. Anna proclaims Him from that moment forward to all who were asking about the "redemption of Jerusalem." In Luke 5, Jesus heals a leper and instructs him to tell no one, yet the very next verse says, "But the news about Him was spreading even farther...." The crowds who witnessed the healing of the paralytic marveled and praised God (also Luke 5). The Gerasene demoniac, now healed, got one of Christ's earliest green lights to tell his story, and he told the "whole city" (Luke 8:26-39).

In healing the ten lepers, Jesus demonstrates His expectation of reaction: *gratitude*. This response was duplicated again and again, including Bartimeus in Luke 18:43.

What should we glean from this? First, that our encounter with Christ produces gratitude. If we are truly aware of the immense debt that's just been lifted from us, an explosive catharsis ought to occur that would take great effort to hide. Second, this awareness of the miracle we've experienced produces in us a yearning to have (at the very least) those we care about experience the same joy.

While our changed life will likely *declare* it, our words *confirm* it (Luke 19:40).

"Confess me"

In Matthew 10:32, Jesus tells us that we who confess Him before men will be confessed by Him before the Father. While verbal confession is not the only manner of communication implied in this statement, neither can it be relegated to secondary status.

In James 3 we learn the tongue is a fire, and the writer bemoans the fact that with the same tongue we praise God and curse men. All of us know too well how human we are: short tempers, words uttered we wish we could take back, sarcastic remarks, and gossip. Those around us, like our co-workers, get ample opportunity to witness this dark side of our tongue. Our verbal silence on our faith creates only one view of us. When these co-workers discover we are Christians, they're left reflecting on only the darker side of our tongue. They attach that impression to our faith.

Ironically, our inability to rein in our sinful nature, especially our tongues, makes us timid about sharing our faith. We worry others will consider us hypocrites, and to avoid that, we simply remain silent. (See the sidebar *Help, I've Blown My Witness at Work* at the end of this chapter.)

Conversely, some of us believe that merely by observing our good works others will see the effect of Christ on our life. The problem is our silence sentences them to seeing only the *effects* of Christ, and not understanding the *source* of those effects: our personal relationship with Him.

Work without verbal assent diminishes impact. Verbal assent without work diminishes the impact, and sometimes destroys it! The two must work in tandem in our lives.

Throughout the remainder of this book, we'll discuss approaches to sharing our faith, like gentle persuasion (chapter 3), when to be silent and *not* share (chapter 4) and reasoning (chapter 9). Not all of us will share the Gospel the same way. It's time, though, to debunk the myth that sharing the Gospel message in our workplace isn't a primary part of our calling. The primacy of evangelism is clear.

If you're trapped on an elevator for hours with others, and you have bread you won't share, they suffer discomfort and you suffer a loss of respect. If you have the Bread of Life, as Christ refers to Himself, and you hoard it, your co-workers suffer far more than discomfort.

What we say reveals our hearts

In Luke 6:49 Jesus talks about the way our words reflect the essence of our being. "The good man out of the good treasure of his heart brings forth what is good; and the evil man out of the evil treasure brings forth what is evil; for his mouth speaks from that which fills his heart."

Eventually, who we are on the inside makes its way outside. We may believe we can mask who we really are to those around us, but eventually what we say reveals our true selves. What does this have to do with evangelism? If we're truly changed by Christ, it will be reflected in the things *we say* and the *way we say them*. If our lives have not been changed by Christ, that, too, is reflected in our words, regardless of our actions.

Managers should rarely be judged by how people outside the organization view them. Rather, they should be measured by how people who work for them view them. Likewise, the words of our guarded moments never truly define us; rather the words we utter in our unguarded moments tell the true story.

Scripture commands us to give verbal testimony

Consider these passages:

Deuteronomy 6:7: "… and you shall teach them diligently to your sons and shall talk of them when you sit in your house and when you walk by the way and when you lie down and when you rise up."

Psalm 37:30: "The mouth of the righteous utters wisdom and his tongue speaks justice."

Psalm 71:24: "My tongue also will utter Thy righteousness all day long.…"

Colossians 3:17: "And whatever you do in word or deed, do all in the name of the Lord Jesus.…"

Romans 10:9,10: "…that if you confess with your mouth Jesus as Lord, and believe in your heart that God raised Him from the dead, you shall be saved. For with the heart man believes, resulting in righteousness, and with the mouth he confesses, resulting in salvation."

Matthew 28:19-20: "Go and make disciples…teaching them to observe all that I commanded you.…"

Do we have to talk? Absolutely.

What we say, and how we say it, now becomes our journey.

IN OTHER WORDS...

Help, I've Blown My Witness at Work

The Apostle Paul likely encountered many people in his missionary travels who were friends and relatives of people he persecuted before He met Christ. Missionary Hans Egede brought European diseases to the people of Greenland he sought to reach with the Gospel, very nearly wiping them out in the process. How did these men face the people they harmed? What prevented them from being disabled by their guilt?

2 Samuel 12:21-23 describes King David after his humiliation in the Bathsheba scandal. The prophet Nathan declares David's sin publicly and tells him of the consequences. Now a child is dead, the direct result of David's actions. David had been praying earnestly for God to relent and spare the child, so much so that his servants were worried he might harm himself when told of the child's death. That's why they were so puzzled when David reacted with calm.

What do we do when we damage our testimony for Christ by our actions or words?

Maybe it's the time we blew up in anger at one of our workers, or at a co-worker. Maybe it's the time we got caught in a lie, or were disciplined for a performance problem. Maybe we've been caught spreading gossip, or trashing the reputation of someone in our office. Maybe our failures were more serious. Most of us at one time or another have been caught in actions that betray our roles as Christians. These inconsistencies cause us to be sheepish, and can sometimes humiliate us. How *should* we handle those moments of faith-failure—when we've damaged the Kingdom of God in the eyes of our co-workers or dishonored God in our actions?

David's pattern in this encounter serves us well. First, we must declare our error candidly. Did you blow up in front of others? Then apologize in front of them also: apologize to them as well as to the object of your wrath. (Don't taint the apology with an excuse.) Second, we must realize that while others are wronged, the sin is against God. "Against you, and you only have I sinned..." says David in Psalm 51. Realizing this truth highlights the importance of restoring our relationship with God even before we attempt to mitigate the consequences of our actions. In other words, we must seek God's forgiveness first.

We should next pray others are spared the consequences of our actions. Ask Him to cause others to see our failure as indeed *our* failure, and not a reflection of the King we serve.

Finally, recognize that sometimes the consequences simply cannot be avoided and must be endured. We must always mourn those consequences, but we can never allow those consequences to so consume us that we cease to be servants in His Creation.

Satan delights not only in the victory of the moment of our failure, but in the spiritual *inactivity* that snares us in our remorse. When we've blown our witness we are humbled, but we must not multiply the damage by retreating into silence and obscurity as ambassadors of Christ.

CHAPTER 3

The Gentle Art of Persuasion

Stormy debates rarely produce decisions for Christ. While we are supposed to boldly declare our faith, the discussion that leads others to explore that faith must be measured and gentle in most instances.

That's one of the reasons "standing up for what we believe" produces so few converts. When we talk about abortion, morality, ethical behavior, and other important matters, lines of battle are often quickly drawn. Both parties take up defensive positions. Christians *should* play a role in those discussions and debates, but rarely in the context of evangelism.

Jesus was a master in the art of gentle persuasion. His approach with the woman of Samaria, whom He greeted at the well in John 4, teaches us much that we can use in the workplace. Even Paul, perhaps the boldest and most candid of the New Testament figures, knew when to be forceful and when to be gentle.

Before we explore some principles of persuasion, we need to identify some assumptions:

1. Most of our co-workers have not read the Bible themselves; any knowledge they have of it is secondhand.
2. Many people who profess to be Christians also have only secondhand knowledge of the contents of the Bible. They get it in sermons, from devotions, in Bible stories—but they seldom get it directly from reading it. Often these professing Christians are the "secondhand sources" of our co-workers.
3. Even those who actually read the Bible can only understand

the message of salvation at first. The "secret decoder ring" for understanding the message of the Bible is a personal relationship with Jesus Christ. With that relationship comes the presence of the Holy Spirit, who moves in our hearts to teach us the full force and effect of all of Scripture. This is an urgent point because a discussion of the Bible between a follower of Christ and someone who is not *will never be on a level playing field. (This assumption is perhaps the most important point workplace Christians must grasp in talking to their co-workers. Don't debate the peripherals, focus on the matter at hand: your concern for their spiritual condition.)*

4. Generally, our co-workers do not naturally *want* to talk about matters of faith. They do, however, have a higher degree of tolerance for listening to our story of faith.
5. Almost universally, people at work are interested in talking about themselves. Therein lies the most important tool in the art of gentle persuasion.

With those assumptions in hand, let's explore the encounter between Jesus and the woman He met in Samaria at the well. As we do, we should see at least five principles of gentle persuasion:

1. People outside the realm of faith are often more easily persuaded than those who consider themselves "good" or "religious."
2. We should know as much as we can about the people in our circle of influence at work.
3. We should incite their curiosity.
4. We should listen well. (See the sidebar *Messing Up the Message* on page 30 at the end of this chapter.)
5. We should answer their questions.

"Would that you were hot or cold…" (REVELATIONS 3:15-16)

People outside the faith are often more readily persuaded to life-changing decisions than those who consider themselves "moral" and "spiritual." Notice the barriers Jesus crossed in His encounter with the woman at the well in Samaria: gender, nationality, doctrine, and even social strata. Why is that important to us as we ponder evangelism in the workplace? Like the Jews of the New Testament who cut themselves off from the Samaritans, we Christians have made the marketplace our modern-day Samaria, the no-man's land of our faith. More often than not, it isn't that our work environment prohibits conversations about faith, it's that we *choose* to edit them out of that part of our lives.

Like the woman of Samaria, our worksites are full of people whose hearts have been prepared by the Holy Spirit for the words of hope we offer. Look at the business publications of the day and you'll see articles on spirituality regularly popping up in their pages. This was true in the 1950s, the 1960s, the 1970s, etc. Interest in spiritual matters may wane, but like business cycles it always returns. This heightened interest creates a field much like the one Jesus had in mind when he declared, "the harvest is plentiful but the laborers are few…pray that the Father will send laborers into His Harvest" (Matthew 9:37-38).

Notice this also about Jesus' ministry: He reserved His stern words for those who were considered spiritually elite, the Pharisees and Jewish officials of His day. With those outside the realm of this religious aristocracy (and even most inside it), Jesus' tone was gentle, humble and compassionate. In our approach to communicating our faith on the job, we must emulate those tones if we want people to listen to the story of Christ. Challenging them on how they're living their life seldom works as a first step. (See the sidebar *Calling Out Christians to Live Differently* on page 32 at the end of this chapter.)

In His encounter with the woman at the well, Jesus moved outside the circle of the comfortable and into the world of the needy.

In our workplaces, our eyes should be open to the outcasts of that environment, recognizing their isolation and extending ourselves to end it.

Know as much as you can about your co-workers

Jesus had an advantage over us in this encounter at the well: he knew ahead of time the woman's story. His revelation of the sordid facts of her life opened her eyes to His words. Why? For one reason, because, knowing the worst, He still spoke to her!

We can't have that supernatural knowledge Jesus did, so we have to get the information by forming a relationship and collecting details of their lives bit by bit. A strange thing happens in this process of data collection: we begin to care about the person, and that caring—that respect—becomes the basis for a proper motivation to share Jesus Christ with them.

This illustrates another important advantage Jesus had over us: He *already* cared about this woman. In our workplace setting, we must *invest* in relationships with our co-workers to get to the place where we care about them temporally and eternally.

For a while in the 1980s, it seemed like every couple my wife and I knew were selling Amway products. In those days couples would invite us over to dinner without revealing we were coming to an Amway presentation, and then follow up dinner with a request for us to become dealers for them. We always found it offensive, and it made us suspicious of every dinner invitation. Eventually, though, we discovered subtle ways to discern the motives behind invitations. Knowing as much as we can about the people we work with should never be a strategy to manipulate them into a conversation about faith. While they may not see it coming, eventually they'll figure out you have them on your "evangelism radar screen" and, absent a relationship, will doubt they are anything more than a statistic to you.

Incite their curiosity

Throughout this conversation, Jesus used the remarks the woman made, or her actions, to generate a curiosity in her. We find her asking questions of Him that probe for more details.

Our discussions with co-workers should also create in them a desire to know more about what we believe. Why don't we work on Sunday? How can we believe in God in the middle of the trials we're facing? How can we believe Jesus is the only way to heaven? While these may be routine pieces of information in our Christian circles, they're a source of curiosity to the non-Christian.

Answers to routine questions like our plans for the weekend offer many opportunities for us to state things in ways that might create curiosity. "I'm teaching a Sunday school class on divorce," or "I'm headed to a men's retreat with my church," etc.—these create openings for the curious to explore. In His discussion with the woman at the well, Jesus paid attention to the details of the encounter and found ways to move her to explore further. That kind of proactive relationship is one we can model with our co-workers without detracting from the job we're doing or creating an uncomfortable atmosphere.

We should listen well

Often our conversations are spent in a one-sided fashion, scarcely waiting until the other person is finished so we can talk—maybe even thinking about what we're going to say instead of hearing what they're saying. People reveal themselves and their interests in extended conversation, and we can glean important clues about them merely by being active listeners.

Jerram Barrs, head of the Francis Schaeffer Institute, advises his students to search for common ground with co-workers, and to begin discussions of faith on those common grounds of agreement. Do they like art? Are they sports fans? Music buffs? Whatever their passion, when we find a common interest the basis for relationship is formed.

From nearly any point of common interest, a part of the story of faith can emerge.

First, we must listen close enough to hear what's behind the words. Jesus stunned the woman with His knowledge of her life. In so doing he captured her full attention. Especially today, people are surprised when we pay attention and retain what we learn about them. When they discover we respect them enough to listen, and care enough to record what we learn, their interest in us is heightened and the relationship is strengthened.

That's only part of the process of listening well, however. The most fruitful discussions we have are those in areas of natural interest to us. Baseball fans can likely quote the current batting averages of their favorite players; music fans can rattle off their favorite songs. They don't need to think about their answers since the information is so much a part of who they are and flows naturally. When we talk about our faith, that must be the case as well. That means we need to be in constant study, so the Bible is a part of our everyday knowledge and the answers to questions (see next section) flow naturally.

Why is that so important? When we reach the stage in a conversation or relationship where someone is interested in exploring faith, our need to listen closely intensifies. What are the real questions they're posing? What are the barriers they're raising? Only when we listen carefully may we know how much or how little to say. However, if we're so unfamiliar with Scripture that we tense up in these discussions, we'll spend our time formulating answers rather than really hearing their questions.

We must answer their questions

Sharing our faith is not a monologue. Sharing our faith is not even a dialogue at first. It is a question and answer session where we answer the questions they're asking and *only* the questions they're asking. When someone asks, "How can a good God let bad things happen?"

our response can't be, "If you only knew Jesus, you'd understand." (No, they wouldn't; but that's another matter.) We must answer their questions.

Conversations about our faith should be driven by the willingness of our co-worker, not by the timeline we set. In a way this is a freeing statement. We don't need to feel like we have to squeeze the whole of Creation, Fall and Redemption into every discussion. There may be times when we get to tell the whole story in one sitting, but those are rare. Rather, we should content ourselves with answering the questions our co-workers ask, and to gradually move them from those questions to the deeper issues.

Often people interested in our faith will test the waters by asking us peripheral questions. If they sense we're coming at them like Bible-thumpers, they'll back off and avoid us like the plague. However, if they discover a measured, honest, well-reasoned response, they'll be more apt to come back for more, especially if our lives and actions echo the answers we give.

Gentle persuasion takes the person from their point of interest to a sense of curiosity and then to a phase of conversation. When the conversation becomes exploration, the real meat of communicating our faith begins.

IN OTHER WORDS...

Messing Up the Message: The Mistakes of Middle Managers

Quality control and quality improvement initiatives broke out of obscurity in the '90s into the world of buzz phrases and fad books. Everyone, it seems, had a strategy for putting quality back into the products America was generating. Much of the effort was genuine, and the fishbone diagram and "80/20 rule" were as common in our lingo as "24/7" is today. (And just as tiresome!)

When the overwhelming majority of these initiatives collapsed, finger-pointing inevitably began. "Management never really meant it!" cried the workers. "The workers weren't committed!" cried the managers. In truth, the failures usually occurred because both employers and employees were not engaged in the effort together. By many estimates, nearly three-quarters of the initiatives launched from the top down failed, in part because the message never reached the lowest layers of the organization, or was edited in the transmission.

Just like Moses' brother Aaron during the Golden Calf incident, failure to deliver the message or protect its integrity—particularly in the absence of the boss—often can be laid at the feet of the second and third tiers of management who skewed what was originally a sincere message of change. Sometimes that skewing was purposeful, but more often it was simply a matter of indifference to the urgency of the message.

So it is with each of us who profess Christ as Lord and Savior. Even adherents of other faiths acknowledge the wisdom and goodness of Christ's words. Not enough! The words must come alive in the message we carry by our actions, our commitment to competence and integrity, and our obvious love for our co-workers. Any day we fail to surrender our efforts to the guidance of the Holy Spirit is a day ripe for messing up the message of God.

Middle managers must be reflective listeners, stating and restating the message from the top before they go out to enact it, so they are sure of consistency in intent and content. They must choose their words carefully, monitor their actions closely, and engage in serious discussion with employees to be certain the message has been transmitted as accurately as possible.

So, too, we who are ambassadors for Christ must be ever listening to that message, stating and restating it to fellow believers as well as in our prayers, and reading it again in His Word—in order to be certain we are representing it accurately and with honor. Then we must choose our words carefully, monitor our actions closely, and engage in serious discussion with those around us to be certain the message has been transmitted accurately.

Being a middle manager is hard work.

So is being a Christian.

IN OTHER WORDS...

Calling Out Christians to Live Differently

Between two armies lies land that neither possesses, where it is unsafe for anyone to find himself...no-man's land. Often the workplace feels like a spiritual no-man's land. On Sundays we seldom hear words about our work; on Mondays we seldom hear words about our faith.

American Christians point to the moral decay of the country and declare its recovery must begin with a return to the morality of the Bible. American men and women in business point to the current crisis in corporate integrity and declare its recovery lies in reclaiming a commitment to ethical behavior in business.

Not so. It begins with you. It begins with me. God is not waiting to hear from Enron or Worldcom's board of directors. He's not expecting the members of Congress to suddenly seek His face. He's waiting to hear from you and me ... and so is the rest of His Creation. *"...and My people, who are called by My name* [that would be 'Christian'] *humble themselves and pray, and seek My face and turn from their wicked ways, then I will hear from heaven, and will forgive their sin and heal their land."* (2 Chronicles 7:14).

Hearing of our faith in this Wise Man, our co-workers look to us for some evidence of the impact of His teaching. Not rote words and harsh judgments; not "be good and God will bless you" paternalism, but real, life-changing, perspective-altering belief! At least some of them are looking wistfully, hoping for some small sign of truth that will mobilize them to leap the chasm from seeker to believer. And what do they see in us? Are we so consumed by the pursuit of success or money (or both) that we're oblivious to their need? Have we so segmented our worlds into work and faith that the twain don't meet, consigning interested spectators to believe Christianity is a weekend disease, insurance against the possibility of the existence of Heaven and Hell?

Are we timid about mentioning our faith to our co-workers? It's time to take a stand, to learn to make what we believe a regular part of our conversations. Are we cutting corners at work? It's time to take a stand, bringing honor to Christ by the intensity, competence and efficiency of the work we do. Are we so consumed by our work that our children's (co-workers, bosses, etc.) souls are neglected? It's time to take a stand, and declare with our words and deeds that Christ changes lives, here and in eternity.

Taking a stand on Sunday morning requires little courage. *It's how we stand in no-man's land* that will mark the impressions of the King we serve in the eyes of those who watch us. We often complain about the perceived silence on faith-work matters from the pulpits, yet we fail to realize our own silence in no-man's land echoes in the canyon of empty souls. Don't complain about silence in one arena and repeat the silence in another!

Our words and our actions must declare "Here I stand!" No other act on our part can quell the confusion of an unbelieving, seeking, troubled world ever watching from the breakfast table, the next cubicle, the next office or the next country.

CHAPTER 4

Learning the Importance of Silence

Are there times when we shouldn't share our faith on the job? Absolutely!

Despite our contention in chapter two that all of us are required to give verbal assent to our faith, we are not suggesting we must do so all the time. In fact, most of our time at work should be spent not talking about our faith. (See chapter eight, "Responsible Workers.")

In particular, there are four categories of circumstances when silence is more important than what we might say about our faith. From the list below, we'll describe the first two briefly and deal with them in expanded fashion in other chapters. Our focus in this chapter will be on the last two points.

1. When talking about our faith distracts us or our co-workers from the task at hand, we should stay focused on that task.
2. When our co-workers aren't interested, we should stop pressing.
3. In the face of ridicule or insincere challenges to our faith, silence is usually the best response.
4. When an answer to one question will move the discussion down a rabbit trail and away from Christ, we should avoid the rabbit trail and wait for the conversation to regain its focus, or redirect the conversation.

The task at hand

We will cover this as a separate topic in chapter eight, but it needs mentioning here. Our employers rightfully expect our attention to be on the jobs they are paying us to do. If discussions about our faith detract from what we or our co-workers need to be doing, then it's not only a bad decision, it's wrong. Hardcore evangelicals will likely be a bit uncomfortable with that statement, which is why we explore it more thoroughly in chapter eight.

"Not interested"

A few years ago, a zealous Christian broke into a dying patient's hospital room to share the Gospel against the wishes of the patient and the family. It caused immense pain for the family, cementing horrible stereotypes in their minds during their grief. Hospital staff who were present were also deeply affected. Though well meaning, that single act did great harm to the work of other Christians in that hospital and in the community at large.

While not all inappropriate evangelistic efforts are so dramatic, the ripple effects are the same. When someone tells us they're not interested in hearing about our faith, we should in almost every instance refrain from pressing the issue. No amount of pressing is going to break into a heart not yet prepared by the Holy Spirit, and few such attempts will turn around someone who is refusing the work of the Spirit. Instead of pressing, we should instead concentrate on representing Christ with competence and integrity while the Holy Spirit works on the lives of those around us.

Silence in the face of ridicule and frivolous challenges

Sometimes our co-workers, and even the work environment, are hostile to our faith. Our stance on business ethics may be different, or on personal moral issues, or on pressing social issues. Some are offended by the exclusive claim that only through Jesus Christ can salvation (and Heaven) be attained. Christian workers retain the same freedoms of expression in these matters as other workers do. Standing up for what's right and doing the right thing are parts of our witness. In fact, informed debate with those who disagree with us sometimes influences others for Christ when we temper that debate with compassion and principles of Scripture.

Often, however, we allow ourselves to be goaded into emotional battles and debates. Frequently these debates are with co-workers whose only interest is in confusing, frustrating, irritating or embarrassing us. Their questions aren't sincere and their purpose is to discredit us and amuse themselves.

Jesus met many of the same kind of people in His time on earth, and seeing their heart refused to be drawn into their games. Indeed, as we'll see in the next section, He was always able to keep His focus on the main issue: His role in the Redemption story.

We must be "wise as serpents and gentle as doves," discerning the legitimate conversations from the distractions, not only for our own spiritual well being, but also because of the audience of other co-workers who inevitably witness these rhetorical battles.

Don't get distracted

For a brief period (three months) I tried selling life insurance. Now don't misunderstand me: I'm certain life insurance sales can be an honorable profession because I know many honorable Christian life insurance sales reps. But I'm one of those people who couldn't sell popsicles to desert dwellers.

During my training for this sales job, I was required to cold-call friends and family members with the intention of selling them policies. Inevitably, I'd get them on the line with a carefully crafted script in front of me. In nearly every instance, though, I would grab at the chance to chase rabbit trails in our phone calls, and never get around to selling any product. We would hang up, and I'm sure they were puzzled by my willingness to talk so long about the frequency of gall bladder attacks in Montana, or the texture of Missouri mud. Most of them never knew how close they were to "securing the financial well-being of those they leave behind."

As Christians we often do the same thing with our co-workers. Because we've been conditioned to believe (wrongly) that faith is a private matter, we don't integrate it into the fabric of our lives or our discussions. That's especially true on the job, where peer pressure and even some policy manuals contribute to this impression.

That means we often approach talking to a co-worker about God the way I approached selling life insurance—with great trepidation. It also means we allow ourselves to be easily diverted from the heart of the matter—Jesus as Savior—to peripheral issues like doing good, business ethics or even doctrinal issues.

Jesus knew how to stay focused on the important matters, even in the times of his greatest distress. Take, for example, His appearance before the high priest on the night of His arrest (Matthew 26:57-63). After His arrest Jesus was taken to Caiaphas where the Jewish authorities tried to recruit false testimony against Him. Throughout the attempt Jesus remained silent. He realized any response by Him would have little impact on His questioners.

When a witness finally did come forward he misquoted Jesus, testifying that Jesus claimed He was "able to destroy the temple and to rebuild it in three days." While Jesus might have corrected him, this would have carried the focus of the meeting in a different direction than Jesus knew it needed to go, indeed that it *did* go. Two verses later, the high priest says, "Do you make no answer? I adjure you, by the living God, that you tell us whether you are the Christ, the Son of God?"

Here, then, was the heart of the Gospel! Jesus finally breaks His silence because the important declaration has finally emerged.

In our relationships with co-workers we get many chances to answer peripheral questions about our beliefs. Often those peripheral discussions can lead to serious talks about God. Sometimes, however, when a co-worker begins to feel the need for a decision, they'll try to back away from that decision (their need for Christ) by focusing on side issues. We need to learn what Jesus knew that night in Jerusalem: at the moment of truth, silence often forces the key issue to the surface.

One other point on silence: Sometimes we must be prepared to absorb ridicule and turn the other cheek even when we know we could defend ourselves. This is especially true in the workplace. We're so afraid of looking weak that we'll vigorously defend ourselves or our beliefs in order to battle the impression that Christians are weak. The problem is in doing so we often abandon the compassion of Christ to protect our egos.

Choosing not to debate abortion, not to debate sexual sin, not to debate evolution, often gets us past these symptoms of our world's need for Christ, and back to Christ Himself. Even when we win the office debate, the energy we've spent winning leaves us little strength for evangelizing.

CHAPTER 5

What Must Be Understood, What Must Be Said

Talking about God in today's workplace requires us to communicate clearly in language our co-workers can understand. However, before we can translate the good news of Jesus Christ into words that make sense to others, we must clearly understand the principles ourselves. We must also know the difference between what we understand and what we must say. Not everything we know about our faith can be grasped by someone who lacks the Holy Spirit in his/her life. So, while we must endeavor to understand a great deal about our faith, we must work equally hard to communicate only what can be understood at first.

It is not by chance that four accounts of the life of Christ appear in the New Testament. Taken together, the volume of the writing reminds us Jesus Christ is the central focus not only of the New Testament but also of the entire Bible.

Those four accounts, though, are not included merely to create emphasis. Each one communicates a unique perspective on this pivotal time in human history. Matthew writes his account with a Jewish audience in mind, drawing analogies and offering anecdotes likely to be understood by a people still waiting for the appearance of the Messiah. Luke's account is drafted for people outside the Jewish faith who may have had little understanding of the Messiah, or for the need of one in their own lives. Luke, not being Jewish himself, was in an excellent position to communicate this surprising new concept of the possibility of a personal relationship with God to people who likely never thought such a thing possible. John seems to offer the most personal account of Jesus' life, capturing in his writing the centrality of Christ's love for men and women. It should come as no surprise to us that John is able to write of love with such resonance, since even Scripture describes him as the disciple whom Jesus loved. The Gospel of Mark likely is Peter's version of Jesus' ministry, recorded by his attendant, Mark. (Yes, the very Mark whom Paul expressed disappointment with, leading to a parting of Paul and Barnabas into separate missionary teams.) Mark appears targeted to a Roman audience, taking special care as it does to explain Jewish terms that would be unfamiliar to those readers. Mark is also the most no-nonsense of the Gospels, often sounding like Jack Webb in the old Dragnet television series with his "just the facts" entreaty. It reflects consistency not only with Peter's words recorded elsewhere in the New Testament, but also with Peter's candid and direct style. Notice, for example, the use of the word *immediately* over forty times in Mark.

Why is understanding the unique audiences of the Gospel accounts important? Because one size does not fit all—and it never has. We cannot hit on one way of telling the story of Christ and expect that it will resonate in the hearts of all of our widely diverse contacts in the workplace. Tracts and visual depictions of the need for Christ are useful tools, but they should form only one small part of our toolbox rather than the sole means of communicating the message of salvation.

Talking about God in the twenty-first century workplace means speaking to a diverse audience. While American business culture retains some of its Judeo-Christian background, more and more of our co-workers come from differing cultures. The cultures they were raised in bear little or no resemblance to the roots of Christianity. In order to talk about God with people from those cultures, we must stop assuming they have a basic understanding of even the simplest Christian tenets of faith. In fact, many people raised in the United States are two or more generations removed from ancestors who knew the Bible. They, too, represent a challenge to us as we strive to communicate the message of Christ.

In fact, one could argue that in the four Gospel accounts are four key strategies for speaking to the various cultures of our co-workers:

1. Matthew's writing serves as an effective basis for discussion with co-workers who have some familiarity with the Bible and with Christian history.
2. Mark serves as a no-nonsense presentation to the hard-charging, career-minded person who wants the sound bite version of everything. For this group, even for those were once schooled in Christian culture, their busy lives have taken them light-years from it, and at best they may be said to have a Sunday school story view of the Bible.
3. Luke offers the broadest possible audience resonance, assuming as he does that much of what he writes will be new information to his readers. A professional (Luke was a physician), his writing also communicates simply without being an insult to bright minds.
4. John becomes particularly effective in the lives of people struggling to understand where God can possibly be hiding while so much is going wrong—in their own lives or in the lives of others.

Clearly we've not covered all the cultures we find present in today's workplace, but the principle has been established. Really knowing the person we're talking to in the next cubicle, or the next office, or the next seat in the break room will help us understand which of these approaches to communicating stands the greatest chance of being understood by them.

What are the important pieces of information we need to communicate when talking about God? First, let's differentiate between what we need to understand and what our listeners need to understand. (See the sidebar *Why We Need Christ* at the end of this chapter.)

Let's start with us. Here are four points we believe Christians must grasp as they try to talk to others about their need for Christ. If you've been a Christian for a long time, you may be tempted to skip over this next section, but we urge you to resist that temptation. Apart from the truth that a reminder of the fundamentals is always good for us, our experiences in the field of marketplace ministry reveal that many who think they understand the basics of faith really cannot verbalize them.

God desires relationship with humans

We need to understand that God desires to be in relationship with us. The Westminster Catechism of Faith reminds us that "the chief end of man is to glorify God and enjoy Him forever." For reasons beyond our human ability to comprehend, the Creator of the universe wants to be in relationship with us, wants us to exist with Him now and in eternity. This truth forms the basis for Christ's actions during His time on earth. Often evangelism initiatives stress the need to accept Christ in order to avoid the consequences of Hell, or to enjoy the security and comfort of the presence of the Holy Spirit. However, these are the *results* of the work of Christ, not the *reason* behind it.

Having grown up in a fire-and-brimstone preaching church, I can attest to the effectiveness of such an approach in getting my attention. While many disagree with an emphasis on the judgment of God, very often it is a path the Holy Spirit uses to get the attention of men and women. So we're not disdaining approaches to getting people's attention, but rather we're stressing the need to remember—and to remember to communicate—that the reason we need Christ is because His sacrifice makes it possible for us to once again be in relationship with the Father.

The exclusivity of Christ

Through Jesus Christ, *and only through* Jesus Christ, can someone be restored to a relationship with God that includes eternal life in His presence. In Christian vernacular this is termed "the exclusivity of Christ," and it causes much turmoil even inside the Christian church. Yet Jesus makes it unquestionably evident in John 14:6 when he declares "I am the Way, the Truth and the Life; no man comes to the Father except through me." Any failure on our part to understand this truth means we water down the words of Christ.

Why the urgency of understanding this truth? Every culture struggles in a search for equity, justice, and even truth. Other religions often can be said to do so as well, though their definitions of those terms differ sharply from a Christ-centered understanding of them. In most cultures and religions, behavior forms the basis for gratifying their god; and the things most sought after in life, including a treasured afterlife, hinge on how well we behave. Any deviation from the exclusivity of Christ that includes behavior as a means of earning grace simply mimics the religions created by men and women down through the ages to fill the void only God can fill. We play right into that theological error when we suggest that someone can live a good life and go to heaven, or live a good life and merit Christ's sacrifice. The work of salvation is all Christ's, and His alone. We receive it as a free gift.

People are not basically good

Despite all human evidence to the contrary, the false idea that people are basically good continues to hold a place in our work culture. Paul addresses this directly when he declares in Romans 3:10 "there is none righteous, no not one," and he reiterates in Romans 3:23 where he points out "all have sinned and come short of the glory of God." If you believe people are basically good, or if you communicate that you believe people are basically good, you diminish the need for what Christ did on the cross. You also make it harder for people to examine themselves closely and see clearly the sin in their lives that separates them from God.

The basics of the redemption story

Not everything we understand about the transaction of grace will be understood by those we seek to talk to about it. Indeed, even those making professions of faith in Christ cannot be expected to fully comprehend what's happening in many instances. However, those of us whom God calls on to testify for Him in the workplace have a huge obligation to understand fully the path of events we're moving our co-workers toward. We must know that:

- Sin separates us from God.
- The Holy Spirit makes us aware not only of this separation from God, but also of the sin in our own lives that causes this separation.
- It is not possible for us to make sufficient amends for our past sins to merit a restoration of our relationship with God, nor is it possible for us to sufficiently refrain from sinning to earn a "from this point forward" relationship with God. Holy living, no matter how intently practiced, still leaves us lacking an ability to restore ourselves to God's presence. In short, we cannot save ourselves.
- Hence, we need another to atone for our sins…Jesus Christ. His death and resurrection was the sacrifice necessary to erase the consequences of our sins and restore us to a place where we can experience God. We do not become sinless, but rather we assume the sinless nature of Christ. When God looks at us, he no longer sees our still-faltering sinful selves, but rather he sees Christ in us. In that moment of transformation the Holy Spirit also inhabits our lives, empowering us to change, to grow in our understanding, and beginning in us the work of making us more like Christ.

Now let's shift our focus back to our co-workers. What do we say

What Must Be Understood, What Must Be Said

to them, and when do we say it? An answer can be found, we believe, in the very structure of the New Testament.

Four books—four unique perspectives on the life of Christ—serve as the launching pad for the New Testament. These four accounts then merge seamlessly into Luke's continuing history as he recorded it in the book of Acts. From there a steady stream of information follows which helps us to build on the foundation—the understanding of the work of Christ as recounted in Matthew, Mark, Luke and John. We've already discussed in an earlier chapter that much of the Bible is a mystery to people who don't have the Holy Spirit present in their lives. This is especially true of Paul's epistles and the latter books of the New Testament. While we can mine these books for our own spiritual growth, and for examples of ways to reach others for Christ, they generally should not be used as primers for discussing our faith with our co-workers. In short, we must keep the focus of our efforts to communicate our faith on the author of that faith, Jesus Christ, and on His work of grace as recorded in the first four books of the New Testament.

Sound elementary? Perhaps, but it's precisely the opposite of common practice. More often than not our discussions of faith center on the dos and don'ts, or on emotionally charged ethical and moral debates. People who don't have a relationship with Jesus Christ no longer see the Bible as authoritative, and they will never be able to do so without the work of the Holy Spirit, which begins when they meet Christ. That means the energy we spend trying to convince them about the holiness of a particular issue is most often lost on them. It's an old and trite saying, but true, that to change people's minds usually requires God changing their hearts.

This does not preclude intellectual discussions that argue from Creation itself for belief in God and for the logic of absolute truth. In a later chapter we'll explore how those kinds of intellectual discussions can lead a co-worker to explore the claims of Christ, an exercise that very often leads them to a relationship with Him. It does argue, however, that the *focus* of the message to those in our work world should be their need for Christ, not the rightness of our moral stances.

Once we realize this, we then need to pay attention to where the people in our offices or jobsites are in this journey toward faith. Understanding where they are in the journey will offer clues to conversations that will resonate with them, increasing the likelihood of their listening to more of the story of Christ.

- Are they struggling with lives that aren't working out the way they hoped?
- Are they in the midst of personal or professional failures?
- Are they dissatisfied with life despite having achieved what they set out to achieve?
- Are they searching for something spiritual, but not necessarily exploring Christianity?
- Are they simply curious about why we're different?

Each of these points in their journey of faith helps to identify aspects of Christ's story that can speak to them. Each of these points can also help us identify which of the four Gospel accounts will most likely resonate with where they are in their journey.

Are they completely oblivious, devoid of any sense of their need for God? Then perhaps intellectual discussions are an excellent place to start—exploring the differences between what they think are the key truths of life and what we do. Chapter nine explores these kinds of discussions, but it's important to note here that the object of those discussions is to move a person past the things in their lives that are preventing them from focusing on the eternal need for restoration to God. The objective should never be to win an argument or make a point. In fact, winning such an argument often forces us to sacrifice Christ-like behaviors and demeanors to do so and drives our debate partner further from God.

Very rarely will we get the chance at work to whip out a Bible tract and walk someone through an entire Gospel presentation, if for no other reason than time constraints. Very rarely will we get the chance to recount for someone on our jobs the entire story of what Christ has done in our own lives. This, then, argues for a cumulative telling of the story, built up in tiny bits over many conversations. Yet, it is urgent for us to consciously move them forward through their journey toward faith in a systematic fashion, remembering what we've told them and searching for opportunities to give them more of the total picture. In short, we must concentrate on communicating the central story of Christ above all other aspects of our faith if we are to participate in the work of God in our offices.

IN OTHER WORDS...

Why We Need Christ

Christians know God created the world, and when He did so it was perfect. He also created man and woman, and set them to work naming the creatures in His creation and tending it (Genesis 1:28). However, through the acts of Adam and Eve sin entered the world when they made a conscious decision to disobey God. Every human being since Adam and Eve has also chosen to disobey God and is therefore guilty of sin.

God is holy and must therefore punish sin, not allowing it to remain in His presence, nor having relationship with those who have sinned. In the Old Testament, a complicated ritual of sacrifices was necessary to atone for the sin in the lives of believers in God, but none of those sacrifices had the ability to "save" a person. The term "save" in this context means the ability to pay for their sins in so comprehensive a manner as to allow them to dwell in the presence of God both now and into eternity, their sins not only forgiven but also erased from the memory of God.

To accomplish this, it became necessary for a once-for-all sacrifice, and God sent His Son, Jesus Christ, into the world for this very reason. Jesus was born to a virgin, and was raised by Joseph and Mary until the time came for Him to begin His earthly ministry. He walked the earth, being both man and God, and lived a sinless life. When the authorities sought to crucify Him, the most painful death of its day, they had no understanding they were playing bit parts in the drama of what Christians term the plan of redemption. Jesus Christ not only lived a perfect life, but also died on the cross as a perfect substitute for each of us, paying the price himself for our sins. But that's only part of the story. Three days after His death Jesus was raised from the dead (celebrated by Christians at Easter), forever conquering the stranglehold sin and death have on humans. He spent days with His disciples after His resurrection and then returned to heaven to be with the Father.

The Bible teaches that only those who acknowledge these acts of Jesus Christ can be restored to a relationship with God. Eternal life with Him, that part of our lives which occurs after we die and is usually referred to as being in heaven, is also only possible to achieve by acknowledging Jesus Christ as Savior by virtue of His death and resurrection.

Part and parcel with this acknowledgement must come a desire on the part of the believer to turn away from the sin that is in their lives and to be forgiven for it. While this does not mean they will be perfect, it does mean they accept that Jesus Christ has first claim on their actions and behaviors, and that making Him Lord of their life is to surrender their sinful natures to change wrought by His power.

Christians further understand that the Bible teaches the Holy Spirit is given to each of us who acknowledge Jesus Christ as Lord and Savior, and it is that Spirit which enables us to live the kind of lives which bring glory to God.

If you are not a professing Christian who believes the things we've described above, and are interested in knowing more about the Bible and what it has to say about this plan of redemption, then we encourage you to contact us at the Marketplace Network to get your questions answered.

CHAPTER 6

Ready to Give an Answer

Our commuter train couldn't complete the trip to Boston, and we were left to wait for busses. I needed to be in Boston sooner than the bus could get me there. While waiting for an outbound train to take me back to my home so I could drive in, an older man struck up a conversation with me. Obviously troubled, his questions immediately grew deeper when he discovered I was a Christian writer. He climbed on the outbound train with me, and we continued our discussion, only to discover the train stopped short of my destination. When I got off the train, a young well-dressed man in his mid-twenties offered to drive me to my house, and I gladly accepted. I noticed he'd been listening to my earlier conversations. We'd hardly shut the doors to the car when he started in...

"I'm getting married soon," he said, "and I just learned my job's about to end. I guess I knew it could happen, but I don't think I really believed it could happen to me. Anyway, it's made me think about things. I come from a family that's not too much into religion, so I don't know very much. But lately I've been worried about my security. I heard you talking to that other guy on the train, and I wonder... *['Please Lord, not now, I've got to go teach a Bible study!' I was thinking to myself as I saw his question coming]* ...can you tell me how a guy can find any real security in this life? *[I knew it! I knew it! I just knew You were going to have him ask me that, Lord!]*"

Our lives are so very busy in this culture there's rarely a good time to have a long conversation. That's particularly true in the workplace where efficiency gurus are driving the idea that fewer workers can be squeezed into doing the same amount of work more used to do.

(Here's an aside from my human resources background: Companies that press for increasing productivity by heaping more work on already overtaxed workers sacrifice research and development ideas that emerge when workers have time to think, as well as time for planning project management. They also increase the likelihood of worker errors, worker injury, and worker illness. Perhaps as damaging is the inability for workers to develop an esprit de corps that serves to meld them into teams far more capable of hitting targeted goals than isolated, stressed individuals. But I digress....)

With the pace of our jobs so intense, our opportunities to talk to others about anything, let alone about something as serious as God, are severely constrained. Nevertheless, as my experience that day on the commuter line demonstrates, those opportunities will continually present themselves because God intends for those around us to hear us speak of Him. Perhaps more than ever before, we must be so well-versed in the truths of Scripture that our answers flow out naturally, even quickly at times. This state of being well versed doesn't come easily however. In fact, it cannot come merely by attending church services faithfully. It also cannot come by adding a weekly Bible study and Sunday school class to our schedules, though all three things are desirable, and in the case of church attendance, even essential.

Then how do we get ourselves ready to give an answer at a moment's notice? First, we must believe we can.

I write a weekly online devotion for workplace Christians. The writing blends my experiences as a human resource manager with my seminary training into thoughts on how the Bible addresses our work lives and issues. Recently a reader wrote to me and commented that the devotion was "one even he could have written, and probably better." The writer in me was stirred up, of course, and it occurred to me to let the reader try. The more I pondered the response, though, the more grateful I was for the work of the Holy Spirit. While I don't know if the reader possessed the skills to craft a text for public consumption, there was indeed truth at the heart of his observation: as a follower of Jesus Christ, he, and every other Christian, has access to the Bible and access to understanding the truths it contains. It's a message every Christian needs to hear: you do not need someone to interpret Scripture for you, because the Holy Spirit will reveal its truth as you study it for yourself.

That's why we should cringe when a pastor or teacher says, "Now in order to understand this verse, you must first know the Greek word…." Immediately, half the audience despairs of ever being able to understand Scripture's more complex lessons because they haven't taken Greek.

Hear this message clearly: *Yes, you can understand the Word of God!*

When Jesus Christ became your Savior, the Holy Spirit also entered your life, and serves as the great equalizer. A secretary in Plano, Texas, a wheat farmer in Nebraska, a CEO in Atlanta and a police officer in Nome, Alaska, can all sit down at night and study the Word of God and have its truths revealed to them. The Bible is accessible to all who know Jesus Christ as Savior, and anyone who teaches otherwise is doing you and all who hear them a grave disservice. (We recognize there are still some churches and church leaders who argue that only they are equipped to understand the Bible, and more space is required to refute their claims than this book allows. If you wrestle with this issue, we encourage you to write us at the address in the front of this book, and we'll send you more information on why God wants you to study His Word.)

However, just because you can understand doesn't guarantee you will. That's because most of us refuse to take the time to study the Bible. Despite a plethora of books and resources designed to help us study, we simply refuse to make it a part of our life routine. Our ignorance is most often a result of our laziness.

Hear this message clearly also: *You cannot profess what you do not know!*

Now, assuming you agree you can understand Scripture, and that you want to, how do you move from a level of reading and understanding to where you can describe it confidently to others?

We recommend the following five steps as a way of helping you along that journey.

First, write out for yourself on a piece of paper a personal statement of faith. You may find it easier to begin by studying your church's statement of faith or the Apostle's Creed. The corporate statements of faith identify what those organizations believe are absolute truths from Scripture. While many statements of faith are very detailed, we suggest you start with seven to ten points, including at the very least the seven points most Christian ministries ascribe to, which are reflected in Marketplace Network's own statement. (See the sidebar *MNI Statement of Faith* at the end of this chapter.)

Now you need to write down why you believe those statements. You may be surprised at how hard this is to do. The assignment becomes even more taxing when we recommend you support your arguments with specific Scripture passages that illustrate your points. Be careful here, though, because you don't want to take a Bible passage out of its context. This exercise will highlight parts of your faith that you need to examine more closely. If you cannot describe why you believe what you believe to yourself, you will not convincingly describe it to someone else.

Once you understand the major components of your faith, keep going; knowing why we believe is immensely comforting when the circumstances of life seem to argue against those truths. More important, though, is that as you study to explain to your *own* satisfaction why you believe what you believe, your new-found confidence in truth will find its way naturally into the conversations you have with those God gives you spiritual responsibilities for, from family members to co-workers.

Second, resist the temptation to let devotions replace Bible study. In my quiet times of study and reflection, I often use Oswald Chamber's marvelous book, *My Utmost for His Highest.* Chambers is so well aware of the frailties of our human response to God that it often feels like he's been watching our lives as he writes his thoughts.

Despite the wonder and power of his writing, it's a mistake to let it replace a close reading of Scripture ourselves. Chambers, and most other devotional writers, begin with a brief passage of Scripture, then write a meditation to apply that Scripture to our lives. Though a helpful (and highly recommended) tool in our spiritual lives, it can become counterproductive when we surrender to Chambers or anyone else the task of explaining Scripture to us rather than discovering for ourselves what it has to say.

Another danger of devotions is their use of "shortcut terminology." Writers constantly struggle to use terms that communicate to the culture of their day, but our Christian vocabulary is so much a part of who we are that we often slip into the language of faith. For example, a writing that refers to the "process of sanctification" often escapes the understanding of many Christians today. (That may be a sad commentary on the state of our spiritual growth, but it's still a fact that needs acknowledgement.) Particularly when we are in the early stages of spiritual growth, we must endeavor to hear more of Scripture directly from the Bible itself, and less of it from secondhand sources, regardless of how strong these sources may be.

Third, consider themed studies as a means of experiencing the Bible. Written Bible studies are an exceptional tool for developing our skills in reading and understanding God's Word. In selecting studies, though, be careful to choose those that lead you into your own discovery. Is there an area of your statement of faith that puzzles you? Check out Christian stores and online sellers for a competent Bible study on the topic. Your pastor or an elder in your church can direct you to authors they have confidence in until you discover writers who treat God's Word carefully and accurately. Working Christians may find that studies that target their workplace issues hold their attention more by intersecting the Bible with the place they spend most of their waking hours. Marketplace Network offers a series entitled *30 Moments Christians Face in the Workplace,* and a growing number of other marketplace ministries also offer Bible study tools on work/faith issues. The goal here isn't to sell Bible studies, but rather to find an area that holds your interest long enough to demonstrate the Bible's relevance to your everyday life, and to help you establish a routine of interacting closely with Scripture.

Fourth, examine the writings of men and women whose writings stand the test of time and truth. The word apologetics is used to describe writings that explain or prove the truth of Christian doctrines. These writings are especially helpful for Christians in the workplace because they offer concrete answers to some of the toughest questions we're likely to hear from our co-workers. Norman Geisler's *When Critics Ask: A Popular Handbook on Bible Difficulties* and *When Skeptics Ask: A Handbook of Christian Evidences* are two examples of apologetics works, but there are many others. Francis Schaeffer, C. S. Lewis, Alister McGrath (professionals may want to examine his book *Intellectuals Don't Need God, and Other Myths of the Modern World*), Paul Little (don't miss his classic work *Know Why You Believe*), Peter Kreeft, Josh McDowell, G. K. Chesterton, Lee Strobel, Chuck Colson, and Ravi Zacharias are just some of the authors we recommend.

In order to make their defenses of faith your own, be sure you read their works with the Bible nearby. Though these authors are terrific, you must still read and discover for yourself the reason and truthfulness of their arguments.

Finally, realize there's very little reason to be surprised by the tough questions your co-workers will ask you. Remember Solomon and his observation "there's nothing new under the sun"? The tough questions of today are the same tough questions Christians have been asked, and indeed have been asking themselves, for centuries. *Why does a good*

God let... Where was God when my... How can the native in the South Sea Islands who has never heard the Gospel... What must I do to be saved... Do you really believe God created... Why only Jesus... Aren't we all really worshipping the same God... and so on.

Many people find journaling to be a productive part of their spiritual lives. If you journal, you'll often discover the tough questions are part of the daily lessons you learn in your relationship with God. The journal, then, becomes a reference tool for use when others face similar circumstances or questions.

Sit down and build a list of the tough questions you'd like answered yourself. This is likely very close to the list of questions you will eventually face as your co-workers become more aware of your faith. Discovering the answers to those questions will not only strengthen your faith, but will also equip you to speak intelligently in the real world of the workplace. (Parents, this exercise is one of the best ways we know of to pass on your faith to your children. By teaching them not only what we believe, but why we believe it, and by offering them answers to the tough questions even before they ask them, we instill in them an innate confidence in the Word of God that most of us spend our lives struggling to obtain.)

One final note of warning. Avoid showing off your newfound knowledge. Remember from our earlier chapters that people without Christ are not able to fully understand the truths of Scripture. While it's terrific to offer pertinent answers to their questions, we must never forget our objective is to steer them back to the story of Christ. Every answer we give on the tough issues should leave a path to Christ open in its answer. We know of many Christians who can defend their faith admirably but never guide their listeners past an admiration of their biblical acumen. Knowledge is important, spiritual growth is desirable, but the story of God is about relationship.

Few works make this as clear as the *Billy Graham Workers Handbook*, a tool used to train the phone volunteers who field calls after a televised Billy Graham gathering. In intriguing, pointed and often poignant ways, the book demonstrates vividly the way to answer hard questions while keeping a personal relationship with Jesus Christ at the center of the purpose of the communication.

We do well to mimic that book in the faith conversations that take place on the job.

IN OTHER WORDS...

Marketplace Network, Inc. Basis of Faith

WE BELIEVE THAT:

The sixty-six canonical books of the Bible as originally written were inspired of God, hence free from error. They constitute the only infallible guide in faith and practice.

There is one God, the Creator and Preserver of all things, infinite in being and perfection. He exists eternally in three Persons; the Father, the Son and the Holy Spirit, who are of one substance and equal in power and glory.

Man, created in the image of God, through disobedience fell from his sinless state at the suggestion of Satan. This fall plunged man into a state of sin and spiritual death, and brought upon the entire race the sentence of eternal death. From this condition man can be saved only by the grace of God, through faith, on the basis of the work of Christ, and by the agency of the Holy Spirit.

The eternally pre-existent Son became incarnate without

human father, by being born of the virgin Mary. Thus in the Lord Jesus Christ divine and human natures were united in one Person, both natures being whole, perfect and distinct. To effect salvation, He lived a sinless life and died on the cross as the sinner's substitute, shedding His blood for the remission of sins. On the third day He rose from the dead in the body which had been laid in the tomb. He ascended to the right hand of the Father, where He performs the ministry of intercession. He shall come again, personally and visibly, to complete His saving work and to consummate the eternal plan of God.

The Holy Spirit is the third Person of the Triune God. He applies to man the work of Christ. By justification and adoption man is given a right standing before God; by regeneration, sanctification and glorification, man's nature is renewed.

The believer, having turned to God in penitent faith in the Lord Jesus Christ is accountable to God for living a life separated from sin and characterized by the fruit of the Spirit. It is his responsibility to contribute by word and deed to the universal spread of the Gospel.

At the end of the age the bodies of the dead shall be raised. The righteous shall enter into full possession of eternal bliss in the presence of God, and the wicked shall be condemned to eternal death.

CHAPTER 7

...Not Forgetting to Pray

Evangelism is a multi-faceted activity. While we as believers are called to give testimony to what the Lord is doing in our lives (and what He did in His act of grace), those are but acts of faithful gratitude. The Holy Spirit works at two levels in our relationships with our co-workers. First, it's the Holy Spirit who softens their hearts, preparing them to hear the testimonies we offer. Remembering this should encourage us, as we realize the supernatural partnership into which we've entered. Second, the Holy Spirit is active in our own efforts, blessing even our most feeble acts when made with a heart of gratitude and a desire to be faithful.

No act on our part is more important than prayer. In this chapter, we want to acknowledge the vital role it plays in our lives, and to make it an important part of our preparation to share our faith. To accomplish this we aim to explore the following:
- Why is prayer important?
- Are there steps to effective prayer?
- Suggestions for praying for your workplace.

Why is prayer important?

Early in the book, we pointed out that many people who call themselves Christians are unfamiliar with the Bible. Annually statistics gathered by the Barna and Gallup organizations illustrate the absence of regular Bible reading and/or study even among those who acknowledge Christ as their Savior. Regular prayer time also suffers in today's hectic pace, and consequently many believers have lost the urgency of prayer.

So why do we pray?

One of the most compelling reasons to do so is to emulate Christ. During His time on earth Jesus illustrated the earthly need to communicate with God through prayer. If we found no other reasons for praying, following the example of Christ would suffice. We find Christ praying in secret (Luke 5:16, Luke 9:18), with others (Luke 11:1), at His baptism (Luke 3:21-22), before selecting his disciples (Luke 6:12-16), and many other times throughout the Bible—including in Gethsemane the night He was betrayed (Luke 22:39) and on the cross when He asked God to forgive his executioners (Luke 23:39-46). In fact, when we read the life of Christ, we find prayer to be one of the most persistent acts of His time on earth.

We were created to be in fellowship with God, and prayer is the most tangible aspect of that relationship. When we read the Old Testament we encounter many examples of this communication between God and humans. Moses, Joshua, Elijah, Nehemiah, Isaiah and all the other heroes of our faith are seen in prayer in the pages of Scripture. Prayer acknowledges our belief not only in God's existence, but in His interest in the details of our lives. We worship Him in our prayers, we beseech His blessing and provision in our prayers, we express our gratitude in our prayers, and we confess our failings in our prayers. Too often, though, prayer becomes a rote exercise which fails to deepen the sense of intimacy we have with God.

The Psalms reflect King David's understanding that we don't need to play mind games with God. Prayer should be an honest, open expression of our hearts, even when our hearts are angry and confused. How often do we pray one thing while we're thinking another? For example, when someone we love is sick, our heart's desire is to see them restored to health. Yet we'll often couch our prayers in holy vernacular, adding phrases like "if it be Your will." Do we really believe God doesn't see our heart? Pray with honesty, and the Holy Spirit will move us from self-centered, "I want" prayer to a place where we can indeed say "Your will be done" and mean it. This integrity in our communication with God breaks down the idea that God only sees and knows what we tell Him. Not only does this make Him more real during our prayer times, but it can also make us more aware of Him throughout our day.

Prayer is also a time for God to speak to us. Christians who pray regularly understand the importance of silence in prayer. No, we're not likely to hear an audible voice giving us play-by-play instructions for the day, but we are likely to sense the urging of the Holy Spirit in the quiet moments. For example, during the "confession" time in our prayers, silence gives the Holy Spirit the opportunity to bring to mind sins we may have ignored or forgotten. At other times, the quiet moments of our prayer life allow the Holy Spirit to place in our thoughts the names of people we should be praying for in that moment.

Though the Bible describes many other reasons why prayer is important (help in avoiding temptation, for example) the final reason we want to point out is prayer's ability to shift our focus from ourselves to our God. When we pray, we actively acknowledge our submissive relationship to the Father, and this action helps to cement this truth in the rest of our lives. Prayer is our recognition that God is in control, and prayers about our efforts to talk about God at work remind us He's in control of that area as well.

Are there steps to effective prayer?

In Christian circles, one pattern of prayer that seems to have gained validation makes use of the acronym ACTS: adoration, confession, thanksgiving and supplication. We would be hard-pressed to argue with the logic of this time-honored pattern. Though we recommend Christians do extensive study on prayer to discover these truths for themselves, we want to discuss briefly the reasons why these steps are important.

Adoration is our acknowledgment of God's holiness, His mercy,

His love and His greatness. When our hearts are obedient, we're able to see and give voice to these truths in our relationship with Him. In the Westminster Catechism, we read at the beginning that "the chief end of man is to glorify God...." Acknowledging His worthiness to receive our praise glorifies Him and prepares us to continue our conversation with Him with the proper perspective. When we list the ways we've seen His holiness during any given day, when we praise Him for the mercy He's shown us by sending His Son to us, when we give verbal testimony to the things we've seen in our lives that are His work, we both glorify Him and place ourselves in submission to Him as we continue to pray.

Confession removes the barrier to our communications. Sin is that barrier, and our confession cleans our hearts and clears our conscience, making our next words intimate in their impact on God and on us. Perhaps in no other part of our prayers is silence so important, giving us the chance to hear the Holy Spirit reminding us of those things we need to bring before the Father's merciful presence.

Thanksgiving is often closely linked to adoration, but there's a subtle difference. Adoration recognizes who God is, while thanksgiving demonstrates our appreciation for what He does in our lives. Adoration places us in proper relationship with God, while thanksgiving reminds us of His faithfulness and our dependence on Him.

Supplication is the time in our prayers when we ask God for the things on our heart. In a concentrated time of prayer where adoration, confession and thanksgiving are expressed, our hearts reach this point, and we now pray with confidence that the things we ask for are heard by God. Note that we didn't say the things we ask for are *appropriate* to be asked for. That implies a perfect-ness in prayer we rarely achieve. Supplication is baring our hearts to God. This act of submission both humbles us and releases us from pretense. As we grow in our spiritual lives, as our practice of prayer becomes more habitual, this final stage of our prayer life also becomes more appropriate.

We learn as we "grow in grace and knowledge" what things our hearts should desire and what things are merely selfish.

Remember also that we pray to the Father through the Holy Spirit, in the name of Jesus Christ. The work of Christ enables us to be in direct relationship with the Father, and the Holy Spirit dwells in us to encourage, enable and strengthen us in that relationship.

One important note. The steps we've described above are for those planned times when we approach quiet time with God. God sees and knows every corner of our lives, and so when the Bible encourages us to pray without ceasing it does so recognizing that no particular process is always possible. In times of danger, for instance, God doesn't wait to see if we've run down the checklist of ACTS before He hears our prayers for protection. In times of deep conviction of sin, God doesn't refuse to forgive us because we forgot to adore Him first. Steps to effective prayer are tools to use in a disciplined prayer life, but God walks with us every moment of the day, able to hear us even in our most hectic moments. Attaching prayer to even mundane times in our lives reminds us of God's presence even there.

In what ways can we pray for our efforts to talk about God at work?

Every mature believer learns over time how to incorporate prayer into every part of their lives. This means you'll discover ways to pray for your co-workers that are unique to your circumstances and profitable to your efforts. What follows are examples of ways *we've* discovered to pray for our workplaces, offered as a way of jump-starting you in your own process of discovery.

Pray over our calendar. Asking God at the beginning of our workday to be with us in our contacts that day helps us discover ways to show them the character of God in those interactions. One of the fringe benefits of this is a reduction in the times we behave inappropriately toward them. Praying for someone has the amazing effect of reducing our animosity toward them. We also often find ourselves reminded of our prayers for them when we see them, and this reminder makes us conscious of their need for Christ.

Pray for those we manage or lead. Scripture defines work as one of the ways we serve God, and this means the people we manage have been placed there not only as corporate responsibilities of ours, but spiritual ones as well. We can pray for God's wisdom in dealing with them, reflecting the character of God in our management styles.

Pray for those who manage or lead us. While our managers have responsibility for us, we as Christians also have an obligation to pray for those in authority over us. Praying for our managers reminds us of their humanity and of their need for Christ. Our hearts can be softened, enabling us to reflect the character of God even in the face of unfair treatment.

Pray for God to make it clear who He wants us to talk to about Him that day, and who would benefit from our silence on matters of faith in that moment. God does not play head games with us. When we seek His direction, His ways will become clear to us, and this includes even the discussions we have about Him on the job.

Divide up the people we pray for into days of the week. Because of insanely hectic paces, the number of people we can effectively, individually pray for is limited. I pray for a different list of people each day of the week. While that often changes based on praying over my calendar, I've discovered this regular pattern of prayer for co-workers and others makes me better able to respond more like Christ during unexpected encounters with them, including times of conflict.

The work of evangelism is the work of the Holy Spirit. The work of evangelism is our work. As the Holy Spirit softens hearts, including our own, so too does prayer change the way we see those who need to hear about salvation.

CHAPTER 8

Responsible Workers

American Christians talk a lot about the restrictions their companies place on their religious activities. In most instances, though, the prohibitions have more to do with the way we talk about God, and not the content. To be blunt, our problem is less about legal or corporate restrictions and more about the offensive ways some Christians bring God up at work. While that statement is likely to rankle some, it needs to be explored in any serious discussion of evangelism on the job.

This smokescreen against evangelism may make us feel comfortable, but it's a paper barrier. Conversations around workplace faith discussions should be centered on correcting our behavior rather than emphasizing the legal prohibitions. Harm is done to the Kingdom when we shirk our responsibilities as employees, especially when evangelism is the reason we do so.

Two areas constitute our focus in this chapter:
- What we can legally do as Christians on the job; and
- Common errors Christians often make in talking about God at work.

What are the legal boundaries for expressing our religious beliefs on the job?

We need to be cautious here, and that's unfortunate. We've become so litigious in our culture that even a Christian document aimed at primarily Christian audiences—such as this one—must be concerned with protecting itself against legal action, even from other Christians. So here's the standard caveat: If you have questions regarding your ability to talk about God in your workplace, we strongly urge you to seek independent legal advice. What we discuss in this chapter are generally acknowledged principles of a Christian's right to religious expression and cannot necessarily be applied to every circumstance.

Having said that, the good news is that there are very few explicit barriers to talking about God in the twenty-first century workplace, despite legend to the contrary. In fact, for those Christians who have a sincerely held belief that their faith requires them to talk to others about God, the Constitution protects that speech and presses the employer to accommodate it. What does that mean, exactly? First, it means we need to examine our own view of Scripture and determine if we sincerely believe God expects us to share our faith in our encounters with those we meet on the job. (Our earlier chapter, "Do I Have to Talk," should give you our opinion on the matter.) This is important, because in any dispute over religious expression at work, an employee will need to demonstrate a sincerely held belief that their faith demands such expression.

So one of the most important steps in establishing your legal right to talk about God at work is an ability to articulate it. In other words, you should be able to demonstrate your belief in Christ's command to "Go therefore and teach…" (Matthew 28:19-20). If you can't express adequately to yourself your understanding of the command to share your faith, it will be difficult to convince anyone else you believe it.

In fact, judging by their silence in the office, it appears most Christians don't believe in the need to share their faith at work.

Once you understand God's command to confess Him publicly, your right to do that becomes protected by the Constitution, within certain limits. These limits include activity that disrupts the normal flow of work on the job, and conversations directed at workers who don't want to have such discussions and who may consider them an imposition, even harassment.

The matter becomes more complex for supervisors, whose exercise of authority over employees makes them more susceptible to charges of pressure, harassment or favoritism. Even in those instances, an employee with a genuinely held belief that his/her faith requires them to talk about it with others may do so, but they must be meticulously aware of not letting it affect their supervisory activities. The matter becomes infinitely more complex in more aggressive evangelistic approaches. For example, if you as a supervisor reach a point where you ask a subordinate to make a decision for Christ, and they refuse, you are more likely to be closely scrutinized by that person around decisions you make which affect them. Additionally, those who are not Christians, and those who are not interested in hearing about your faith, may be watching to see if you reward Christians or those who are willing to listen to you talk about your faith, to the detriment of those who don't.

Most of those who offer advice for talking about God in the workplace recommend you do so during breaks or before and after work begins. As safe as that advice is, it greatly increases our natural tendency toward compartmentalizing our faith so it becomes purely a private matter with little or no impact on our jobs or our co-workers. Such a dichotomy is in direct violation of Scripture. Our faith is part of every aspect of our lives, including the single biggest consumer of our waking hours, the job.

Avoiding this dichotomy forces us to consider carefully the times and places where we do talk about God at work. However, a more effective approach is to make our understanding of Scripture such an integral part of our lives that we begin to express it naturally, in the vernacular of the workplace, but also with a sincerity that makes it apparent it is an essential fiber in the tapestry of our lives.

Our co-workers likely already know we're avid skiers, or rabid Kansas City Royals baseball fans, or fans of *Gone With The Wind*. These aspects of our personal lives weave their way naturally into our conversations and reveal something of us to our co-workers. So, too, can discussions about what we believe, and why we believe it, become natural parts of our discussions—but only if they're truly integrated into our lives in our Bible study and prayer times through persistent and close reading of Scripture.

As we mentioned earlier, however, the real battle isn't over what we legally may or may not do, but over inappropriate ways we might choose to talk about God at work. Christians have an obligation to consider carefully how their words and actions on the job reflect on God. This means every aspect of our work must be taken into account as we fulfill the role Paul reminds us we have as ambassadors for Christ (2 Corinthians 5:20). (See also 1 Peter 3:15.)

What are some of the common errors Christians make on the job?

First, Christians sometimes engage in religious activity when they should be working. Bible reading and conversations about God with co-workers are good things—in their appropriate place and time within the boundaries of the rules of the workplace. However, any of these activities may become harmful to the Kingdom when they displace time and efforts appropriately owed to the task at hand. (See the sidebar *He Also Made Me Fast!* on page 71 at the end of this chapter.)

One of the first missionaries for the African Inland Mission, Willard Hotchkiss, served for forty years in the Kenyan region, breaking new ground for the faith while struggling daily to have enough to eat and to provide for his family and those under his care. Along the way he learned important lessons, one of which is recorded in his book *Then and Now in Kenya Colony* (Fleming Revell, 1937).

> Missionaries are often criticized because their adherents so often divorce religion from life. The charge is true enough, and the missionary is usually the first to recognize the fact and to mourn over it. Nor does it help matters to retort that the same thing is true

of so-called Christians at home. This world will be a different place to live in, when Christ is dominant in the counting house as in the church; when the Spirit of Christ permeates the weekday activities as the Sunday devotions; when the Bible rather than the card deck becomes conspicuous in the home.

… Sometimes I have gone about the mission plantation and have found the young men sitting in the shade of the trees, reading their Bibles. Now no one, least of all a missionary, can be unmoved when he looks on the fruit of his labors. And this was the very thing I had given life for—to teach these people to read the Word of God. But a perfectly good thing may, under certain circumstances, become a bad thing. These lads were being paid to do a job of work. So, instead of commending them, I had to point out that under the circumstances, they were actually dishonoring God by reading His Word. When they took time which belonged to their employer, and used it even to read the Word of God, they were guilty of theft.

We need to establish a background of integrity against which our witness for Christ shines, and one of the first ways to do that is to diligently give our employer and our job the attention they deserve.

Second, Christians often use words to represent Christ when their actions have not earned them a measure of respect. Though not a hard and fast rule, our co-workers will attach much greater credence to the testimony of someone whose work they respect, and whose work ethic is unassailable, than they will attach to that of a newcomer. We're not suggesting timidity when starting a new job, but we do caution Christians to establish themselves as credible and competent employees. This investment in our reputations is an important facet of stewardship of the role God calls us to in our jobs.

Third, our words of faith often sound shrill when they aren't expressed in the context of relationship. Far too often Christians give the impression that the people with whom they talk about God are statistics or checklist items on a chart of religious obedience. Natural discussions about our faith are most comfortably communicated, and most comfortably received, in the context of relationship. People who believe we care about them are less likely to doubt our motives when we talk about God with them.

Fourth, Christians often emphasize the negatives in their discussions about God. A co-worker early in my human resources career told me he had an excellent idea of what God was against by listening to me, but very little idea about what God was *for*. Those words have stayed with me through the years as I remind myself how often we use our faith as a weapon to attack other ideas, or as a sword to defend our own beliefs.

Fifth, Christians often criticize other Christians in front of their co-workers. For a faith that teaches so much about loving our neighbors, it's hard to imagine it has any credibility when its ambassadors are always firing darts at each other. Satan absolutely delights in highlighting the areas where we Christians disagree with one another, and we play right into his hands. Not only do we disagree, but we give voice to that disagreement, often in public venues. What could possibly be attractive to non-Christians about a faith that engenders such visible animosity? Nowhere is this more evident than in so-called doctrinal disputes. We take our disagreements over biblical truth into the public arena, and the nastiness with which we wage those battles not only harms us and those we fight with, but also the witnesses to those fights. Worst of all, we do great harm to the Kingdom of God. We should be ashamed! Even when defending the most important facets of our faith, we must exhibit the character of Christ. (See the sidebar *Shoulder to Shoulder* on page 73 at the end of this chapter.)

Sixth, our knowledge of Scripture is poor. Just as we must be competent in the job, we must be equally competent in our handling of the Scriptures on the job. It is essential we find ways to steep ourselves in the truths of the Bible. Life at work seldom offers us time to run and find a passage of Scripture that applies to the task before us. Rather we must work to commit the truths of the Bible to our minds so they are accessible in the heat of workplace moments. Even in the most boring of our quiet times, God is at work making His Word come alive in us.

As we read the Bible, He begins to work revealing truth to us. He is also faithful to bring those truths forward as we go about the routine tasks of life. *His word will not return empty!* (Isaiah 55:11) Our decisions at work must be guided by those truths, and our culture begins to be influenced by them through us.

Our witness to the goodness of God and the effects of Christ on our lives are easily diminished by careless approaches to integrity, competency and sensitivity. We must be "wise as serpents, but gentle as doves" as we serve on the front lines of His work in our workplaces.

IN OTHER WORDS...

He Also Made Me Fast!

We must stamp the efforts of this day with a competence that is worthy of the God we serve.

> *"I believe God made me for a purpose—for China. But He also made me fast! And when I run, I feel His pleasure. To give that up would be to hold Him in contempt. …to win is to honor Him."*
> – Eric Liddell, film dialogue, *Chariots of Fire*

Eric Liddell never saw winning the Olympic medal as the purpose of His life. His purpose, his life service, would be serving as a missionary, and ultimately a martyr, for the cause of Christ in China. But he understood what few of us in the workplace choose to believe...honoring God is about doing our best in today's work, not waiting for tomorrow's promise. Being competent in the place God has us right now is how we honor Him. Whatever we're doing this day—driving a truck, managing a company, plowing a field, punching a keyboard, tending children—now is the moment God calls us to honor Him.

If a first key step in shaping our workplace is forming a bond with other believers, then a second must surely be *competence in the task before us now.* Developing ourselves into effective and valued workers is a vital building block for influencing our work culture. God may indeed choose to use someone who is not competent to bring glory to Himself. But more often the most effective impact for Christ comes from workers who seek to do their work responsibly and competently, and to honor the time and resources of their employer. We often fail in our efforts to honor God precisely because we fail in honoring our employers.

When an employer, co-worker or customer trusts your daily work efforts, they are more likely to trust your spiritual efforts also.

Eric Liddell won a gold medal in the Olympics, then slipped into the tiny villages of China to serve Christ daily there. "He made me fast!" was but a scene in his life, and he played his role well in many other unseen scenes. He didn't wait to reach China to serve God, but served Him in the circumstance and with the skills God gave Him each moment.

"He also made me _____?" How we complete this sentence defines where we serve Him next. Tomorrow is not the time to be competent. We must do it now.

IN OTHER WORDS...

Shoulder to Shoulder

"**Y**ou have bled with Wallace, *now bleed with me!*"

In this stirring scene from the movie *Braveheart*, Robert the Bruce heads a Scottish army still mourning the death of William Wallace. With these words, even members of movie audiences were ready to jump out of their seats and join the battle.

What is it about humankind that makes us able to offer our lives for ideas of justice and freedom, but fails us when called upon to represent our true King, Jesus Christ? It is largely, I think, because we fail to see our routine daily efforts as part of the "living sacrifice" Paul calls us to in the text from Romans. We must commit ourselves not merely to surviving in the work culture that feeds our family, but to *minister* there, perhaps even to *shape that culture*.

But, how? Where do we start? *Seek out other believers in your workplace and build relationships with them.* An employer once told me he could tell when two of his employees were in love by the "electricity between them." He continued, "I don't sense love between you Christians; you shoot your wounded!" *Christians are often defined not by what binds them together, but rather by what separates them*. The hope that is in us (Christ Jesus) shines ever brighter when bound to others with that same hope! While it's true even one person can make a difference in a culture, its equally true a *team* of people often have better success in accomplishing difficult tasks. Consider these five additional advantages to knowing and respecting other Christians in the workplace:

1. We are able to fellowship, offering encouragement steeped not only in our common Savior, but in our common

understanding of the setting where God calls us to work.

2. We are able to pray for each other with greater insight than are the people outside that particular workforce.

3. We may be able to seek counsel from, and offer counsel to, each other on matters relating to the particular department or company where we work.

4. We are able to hold each other accountable in ways pastors, friends and family members cannot during the workday.

5. There may be opportunities for us to coalesce in shaping or influencing the work culture.

Our world has ample evidence of the bonds of firefighters and other professions. *It is time for you and me to show the bond of the believers,* who hear Christ's words in John 14:1, "…[you] believe in God, believe also in Me." Like the Scottish warriors, may we be moved by His mercy to become living sacrifices every minute of our day.

CHAPTER 9

Come, Let Us Reason Together

Throughout this book we've emphasized the need for a personal relationship with Jesus Christ. We've made it a thread running through the work because of the centrality of Christ not only to salvation, but also to life itself. We have also stressed that without Christ, much of the wisdom of Scripture escapes the understanding of modern men and women—hence our keen desire to see Christians focus on the work of Jesus Christ in their conversations with co-workers.

While a non-Christian may be unwilling to accept Scripture as absolute truth, or to understand the bulk of its teachings, it does not mean we cannot express our faith in logical terms that appeal to a person's intellect. In fact, Christianity has been far too eager to abandon a commitment to the truth of Scripture, to abandon our ability to reasonably explain why our faith is consistent with God's creation, to abandon efforts to describe why our worldview—a Christian worldview—is the only one that makes sense. That willingness to surrender truth and reason to scoffers and humanists only makes it more difficult for thinking people to consider Christ, and worse, makes it more difficult for the next generation to believe in Jesus Christ.

Our tendency to describe what we do as a leap of faith suggests there is no logic to it. It further suggests we must suspend our rational selves in order to participate in the spiritual.

In his classic apologetic work *How Then Shall We Live*, Francis Schaeffer attacked such notions effectively. Years later, Chuck Colson resurrected his thinking with his own apologetics work, written with Nancy Pearcey, *How Now Shall We Live*. Marketplace Christians will find both these volumes invaluable tools in recapturing a sense that Christianity is *reasonable* even in the face of a skeptical, pseudo-scientific world. It also holds together in the face of a scientific world. More to the point, in a world of bottom-line measurement, the absolute truths of Scripture may be relied on as the final authority for every area of life, including the workplace.

Modern men seek to escape the limits created by belief in moral absolutes. They seek to escape responsibility for their actions by suggesting that differing circumstances alter the line between right and wrong. Yet, to challenge moral absolutes, human beings must force their way past the idea of a holy God. Finding it difficult, if not impossible, to argue against some moral certainties in the Bible (murder, lying, theft, cheating), they must attribute those moral certainties to a universal truth because failure to do so would force them to have to seriously account for other moral absolutes in Scripture.

In fact, finding it intolerable to have moral barriers, humans have sought to challenge the very existence of God. Their most effective partners in this dismantling of the grounds for a belief in absolute truth have been a scientific community often ready to allow its work to be used to discredit faith, and generations of Christians willing to abandon the intellect in their exploration and embracing of faith.

When the telegraph was invented, one writer recorded his certainty that humans would never again discover faster ways to communicate. While we chuckle at the naiveté of that statement, it's been echoed in modern-day observations of instant messaging on computers. What science declares to be absolutely certain in one generation often is upended in another.

Colson demonstrates this effectively in his apologetics work by building on the basic laws of physics. The first law of thermodynamics says that the total quantity of energy in the universe remains constant.

This is the principle of the conservation of energy. The second law of thermodynamics states that the quality of this energy is degraded irreversibly. This is the principle of the degradation of energy. Scientists for years have maintained the eternality of the universe, basing it on the first law of thermodynamics, that matter cannot be destroyed. Because matter cannot be destroyed, it must always have existed, they posit, and hence the idea of a single act of Creation simply cannot be. As Colson points out, the same law of thermodynamics that argues the permanence of matter implies it cannot just appear or create itself. In other words, if it could be demonstrated the universe has a beginning, then something external would have to be responsible for its existence. Colson continues to press the point by identifying what scientists term the second law of thermodynamics, the so-called law of decay. For decades now, science has reluctantly acknowledged the universe is "winding down," as Colson says it, toward a period of darkness and ultimate decay. Taken together, the two laws themselves press for acknowledgement of a beginning, and one not explained by a theory of matter creating matter. Something, or Someone, external to the natural universe necessarily is responsible for that beginning.

In fact, the theory du jour, the Big Bang, accepts the idea of a beginning, dismantling decades of "scientific certainty" that a point-in-time beginning to the universe was not possible. (Don't read into this sentence an endorsement of the Big Bang theory.) Scientific certainty is often attached to matters which seem to contradict our faith, but Christians can and should be encouraged by the frequency with which science, and even historians, are forced to return to Scripture and acknowledge its truth when their human pursuit of "certainties" fails to stand the test of time.

Despite their professions of belief in absolute truth, however, Christians avoid intellectual examination of scientific, intellectual and even cultural challenges to the truths of Scripture. It's possible many do this out of fear it might shake their faith, and so they close their minds and hold on "by faith" to the hope that what they believe is true. Some do it because they believe themselves incapable of grasping the arguments. While this failure doesn't threaten the salvation of the believer, it severely limits their witness to the truths of Christ they can attest to in their lives. It also makes conversations with co-workers who honestly seek answers to life's questions wholly unsatisfying for both the Christian and the inquisitor. The timidity and doubt of the Christian, when measured against the bullying confidence of humanists or naturalists, makes it difficult for those exploring matters of faith to take seriously even the Gospel account—the one part of Scripture accessible to them.

Even more devastating, when we as Christians surrender to a "leap of faith" standard for accepting Scripture, we leave our children and new Christians defenseless when their faith is challenged.

The manipulation of science has been destructive to human acceptance of God's Word as absolute truth. However, it was attacks from inside the believing community that separated Americans from a confidence in the Bible. Self-proclaimed theologians and scholars, particularly in the nineteenth century, began to attack the authenticity, the accuracy and the authority of the Bible. They did it by challenging the historicity of Scripture, the scientific reliability of Scripture, the authors of Scripture and even the concept of supernatural inspiration of Scripture. With science attacking Creation from the outside and pockets of theologians assaulting it from the inside, Christianity's response was often to throw its hands up over its head to hide. This retreat from the search for truth surrendered the classrooms, the podiums, the press and in many instances even the pulpits, to the enemies of absolute truth.

Under this cultural barrage, Christians retreated further, questioning *rationality* and suggesting instead a need to suspend the rational in order to believe God.

This retreat manifests itself today as rampant uncertainty on the part of the average Christian as to the accuracy, the authenticity and indeed even the authority of Scripture. Unfortunately, we cannot have it both ways. Either the whole of Scripture is truth, or none of it may be relied on with certainty. Those who would challenge part of Scripture necessarily void their ability to rely on the rest of it.

What does this mean for the marketplace Christian? It means we must make our faith a part of our entire being, exploring it intellectually as we experience it in our relationship with God. The hard questions we fail to answer for ourselves are the hard questions our co-workers often want to ask us, and our inability to address them makes our God seem like fantasy, not the reality we know Him to be.

It means we must confront the doubts we have about the accuracy of Scripture head on, studying it closely to see how it overcomes the false charges of inconsistency, contradiction and inaccuracy. Rather than being afraid of what such a journey might uncover, our confidence in God as the author of truth should cause us to set out on that journey in boldness.

Such a journey also provides us with terrific discussion material at work. The deep issues of life are universal questions, and our ability to speak authoritatively on them to career-minded co-workers who consider themselves enlightened is a powerful icebreaker on the path to telling them about Christ.

Two reminders close this chapter. First, we must never forget, even as we endeavor to understand the logic and the rationality of belief in God and His Word, that *relationship* trumps *intellect* in the Kingdom of God. The chief end of man is to glorify God and enjoy Him forever. It is not merely an intellectual assent of the existence of God that is the object of our faith: it is to be restored to relationship with Him. *Knowing* must never be abandoned, *doing* must never be diminished, but *being in relationship with Him* is of primary importance.

The second reminder is simply that even the ability to debate the deep questions of life must be viewed, as Francis Schaeffer termed it, as pre-evangelism, restoring a person to a place where Christ can be seriously considered. While we must always be aware that the Holy Spirit draws them to God, we have been selected to participate in that process through the commands of Scripture to tell others about Jesus Christ.

CHAPTER 10

What If They Say Yes?!

Paul and Silas could have escaped.

Wrongly imprisoned, an earthquake shook the foundations of their prison, broke open the doors and loosed the chains holding them. So certain was the jailer they had escaped that he prepared to commit suicide. Paul stopped him, and the jailer's reaction was sweet music to the Apostle's ears (Acts 16:22-40): "Sirs, what must I do to be saved?"

How very rare those words are in our culture today. Yet they point to the certainty that God does indeed draw to Himself people in our circles of influence. When that occurs, when a person responds to Christ and looks to us for guidance in the next steps of the journey of faith, what should we do?

First, we must understand the urgent importance of fellowship and community at that point in their spiritual journey. Particularly in the case of the workplace, someone who comes to know Christ as their Savior is likely to experience changes that will affect their work relationships. Some will lose friends because of those changes; others may even need to change jobs. This sudden earthquake in their spiritual world is paralleled by tremors in their physical world. Hit and run evangelism, which moves on to the next "victim" once we "slide another soul inside the pearly gates" often leaves the new believer bewildered and uncomfortable. Immediately following conversion, we need to move alongside new believers to help them understand the changes they are experiencing.

We also need to help them find a church, where they can begin to understand the importance of the Body of Christ in their spiritual growth. Even when we're able to spend large blocks of time with a young believer, the blessings of being in a community of believers are immeasurable. Just seeing and knowing other intelligent people embrace faith is an encouragement.

For those whom God places in our path, we share a responsibility not only to tell them about Christ, but also to help them in their spiritual journey after they receive Him. This is commonly referred to as discipleship. But how do we help them grow? What goals should we be working toward as we help them understand this life of faith?

In an old book on missionary preparation, Roland Hogben outlines principles he considered necessary to the success of a missionary. We believe they also serve as challenging goals for discipling relationships to achieve in the life of the one being discipled. Consider these five goals:

1. A life yielded to God and controlled by His Spirit.
2. A restful trust in God for the supply of all needs.
3. A sympathetic spirit and a willingness to take a lowly place.
4. Love for communion with God and for the study of His Word.
5. Some experience and blessing in the Lord's work at home.

We've spent time in earlier chapters discussing the first and fourth points. Suffice it to say here that the first point does not come naturally, but must be emphasized as the new believer learns what it means for Christ to be not only Savior but Lord in his/her life. As we've said frequently throughout this book, the practice of number four is the only sure path to achieving number one.

Perhaps none speaks so poignantly to the iron grip this world has on us than the second one, that God can be trusted to supply all of our needs. In an age where profit has been placed on a throne, where shareholder return is used as an excuse for dismantling factories and destroying lives, where job security is perceived as a fatality of our culture, many marketplace Christians are immobilized by the fear of a lack of provision. This fear causes knee-jerk reactions—from simple ones like working long hours to impress a boss, to complex and dangerous ones, like agreeing to participate in unethical, even illegal behavior in order to keep a job. But the time to teach this lesson is seldom after one has entered the marketplace. Like the missionary heading overseas, there must be a pre-existent awareness of and confidence in God's ability to provide. If we understand we're in the marketplace to do God's work, then we must prepare for that ministry as the missionaries do. This ability to lean on God removes many barriers for us, though certainly not all of them, and yet it is a fundamental struggle for most marketplace Christians I know. Establishing this as a principle in the life of a new believer is a gift that will pay dividends for the rest of their careers.

How can we not admire a call to "a sympathetic spirit and a willingness to take a lowly place?" For most of us, life is a ladder, and our energies are spent in reaching for that next rung, either measured by financial success or accomplishment. For the missionary, however, there is the sense that he/she is headed off to a remote part of the world where even family members will not have a keen idea or appreciation of their daily contribution to the Kingdom, and where little of the world's marks of success will be within their reach. It is a question of sacrifice, a vital concept we must introduce into the training of Christians who select careers that take them into the dog-eat-dog world of the marketplace. In a world of competition, we've somehow decided that shoving ourselves into the fast track is the only way to achieve success. So, we consign our unused gifts and talents to the wastebasket of our lives in order to keep pace with the perceptions of success on the world's terms. "Someday…" we promise ourselves, thinking we'll find time to be who we were created to be when we've achieved security or success on the world's terms. For many of us, "someday" never comes, smothered by our inability to see that the ladder of success is very often really a treadmill. (We aren't suggesting success is inherently bad, but success in any endeavor must be viewed in the context of God's claim on our lives.)

Oh, we may do our roles competently, but the stress of working outside our God-given design makes other parts of our lives difficult, even untenable, especially for those around us.

We like to blame the managers. The truth is, though, we often choose to be used out of sync because it fits the objectives we've set for ourselves apart from God. We want to matter, we want to be significant, we want more money, we want more power, we want security, we want more leisure, we want…WE want…. There's an emphasis on *we* that violates our relationship with God.

I am an accountant because… I am a truck driver because… I am a CFO because… I am a legal secretary because…

Answering those questions candidly requires a careful look at our lives and our motivations. It also requires a careful look at how God designed us, where He's at work, and what role He wants us to play in the place where He's working. We have to ask questions like "How does God define success in my life?" and "How much (money, power, security, etc.) is enough?" and "How does how He made me relate to the real world of job selection, and even whether or not to accept a promotion?"

We choose to be used every day. Sometimes we choose to be used by our jobs, sometimes by other people, but more often we choose to be used by our own wants. It's time we choose to be used by God, in the place where He wants us. For some, that may mean staying right where we are and merely changing the reason we do what we do. For others, it may mean acknowledging it's time to make changes that are more dramatic. This important lesson, often not yet appropriated in our own lives, is an important truth to instill in the new believer.

We must also pay particular attention to the final item, experience and blessing in the Lord's work at home. Here, the local church plays a key role in the life of the workplace Christian. If the new believer (or even the mature believer, for that matter) fails to see and experience the impact Christ has on our church and its members, there is little chance that they will be able to create it in the workplace. The truth, then, is that ministry in the marketplace has at its root a need to replicate, not create. We are to replicate Christ's impact on our lives, and to replicate the sense of caring and community that His impact has on our church, and in order to do so, we must witness it in places outside the marketplace.

Companion Studies

COMPANION STUDY FOR CHAPTER 1,
"WHY BOTHER?"

Following Philip—Going Where We're Led

(Acts 8:4-40)

Among workplace Christians few topics create more angst than discussions around sharing their faith at work. Some find the matter offensive, conjuring up images of water-cooler evangelists passing out tracts and pouncing on unsuspecting passersby. Others find it frightening, worried they'll say the wrong thing or that it will adversely affect how their co-workers view them. Most simply don't see how they could do it, and don't know where to look to learn how.

Describe some places where people might be expected to hear the Gospel message in our society today.

Which of these places require action by a person *before* they can be confronted by the Gospel message?

What does that suggest about the vast majority of the people in our workplace?

In the days of the early Church, much of the world was not in a position to hear or see Jesus during His time on earth. Why do you think that's true?

What about Samaria? Using a Bible commentary or a study Bible, try to discover why Samaria would still be off-limits to the Jewish follower of Jesus Christ. What are the parallels between the people in your workplace and the Samaritans?

Now read Matthew 28:19-20 with a pencil. Record below the places Jesus described as needing to be reached with the Gospel as He commissioned His followers:

In particular, pay attention to "Samaria" and "the uttermost parts of the earth" as we explore Philip's journey.

Read Acts 8:4-25 and briefly describe the reaction of the Samaritans to Philip's ministry.

With Paul being prepared to carry the Gospel beyond the Jewish people to the Gentiles, and with Peter and other Apostles carrying the Gospel to the Jewish people themselves, Philip becomes a key figure in completing the commission Jesus described in Matthew 28 above.

Study Acts 8:14-16. What occurs in these passages, and how might it relate to our efforts in the workplace? How might it relate to the organized Church's response to our efforts? Why is that important?

Now look at Acts 8:25-40. Read the passage through once first, as an overview. Look closely at verses 30 and 31. Is there a more poignant statement in Scripture? Think of your co-workers: What are some of the books they're reading as they search for wisdom for the workplace?

Why are these books so popular?

Name some of the barriers you and your co-workers run into as you read the Bible? Compare those barriers to the ones we see here in Samaria and with the Ethiopian eunuch's response.

How did Philip help? What role does that suggest for us? (For deeper study, consider how we prepare for that role.)

Now look at verses 26 and 29. Why did Philip go to Samaria and do what He did? Describe what that might mean for your selection of a workplace or career.

Finally, note this: In both Samaria and "uttermost parts of the earth," which is where the Ethiopian eunuch's home was, the Gospel was carried not by the established Church, but by one of its members venturing forth. What does that suggest in your work life?

Describe the fruits of Philip's labors in both places. How would you think he measured success?

We live in a culture which has become immune to the Bible, scarcely even aware of its truth, and only marginally aware of its story or theme—Creation, Fall, Redemption. Read Acts 8:31 and Romans 10:15ff. Describe why these verses can be used as a motivation for fulfilling the Great Commission in Matthew 28:19-20.

Finally, let's look at a few additional reasons why we should bother to share our faith on the job.
Read Matthew 25:41-46, Matthew 8:12, Matthew 5:29-30, 2 Thessalonians 1:9, and Rev. 19:20. What motive might these passages suggest? What's the resistance to this motive in today's culture?

Read John 14:6. With all the self-help books, all the positive-thinking gurus, all the do-good-and-go-to-heaven works out there, why is this verse so central to what we must share with our co-workers?

Consider Matthew 28:19-20. Is this a request? To whom does this passage refer, and how does it apply to our workplace?

Now read Acts 8:11, Acts 8:38 and especially John 4:39-42. Why might this motivate you and me to share our faith with our co-workers? What might the potential outcome look like?

COMPANION STUDY FOR CHAPTER 2,
"DO I HAVE TO TALK?"

No Longer "Not Yet"

Saint Francis of Assisi is credited with saying, "Preach the Gospel always, and, if necessary, use words." Many Christians latch onto this expression and attach almost biblical status to it. More often than not, they're doing so because they don't want to feel obligated to give verbal assent of their faith.

In our first study we listed some of the places (like church, Billy Graham events, etc.) where people might hear the Gospel message. Realizing many of our co-workers will never make it to these events, where might they be expected to hear someone verbally describe what is necessary for salvation?

Do you believe it is essential for us to give verbal assent to our faith in the workplace? Why or why not?

Examine the following Scriptures. As you consider the question of the need to talk about God, what pattern do you see in these passages?

Luke 2:8-20

Luke 2:25-35

Luke 2:36-38

Luke 5:12-15

Luke 5:18-26

Luke 18:35-43

How do the experiences and responses of these people who met Christ compare with your response when you first met Christ? How do their responses compare with your present attitude toward Christ?

Study Luke 17:11-19 in light of your own spiritual response to the work of Christ in your life. Which of the two groups of lepers most closely resembles your current response?

What are some of the reasons for this in your life?

For a second reason why verbal assent is important, read Matthew 10:32. What relevance could this verse have as we ponder talking about God in the twenty-first century workplace? How does this verse support the idea that verbal assent is essential in the Christian's life?

In Luke 6:49 we discover more information about why words are important. In thinking about this verse, list the three things you talk about most with your co-workers that are not work-related:

1.
2.
3.

Now describe the most common attitude your co-workers or customers see reflected in your conversations. In what situations are you most often critical? In what ways are you viewed as a debater? Using as candid a self-assessment as possible, how do you think your co-workers would describe your heart purely from listening to your words?

Read Luke 6:49 again with this description in mind. What role could a verbal assent of Christ play in changing their perspective of your heart? What role could a verbal assent of Christ play in changing your heart?

Next, examine these Scriptures for clues to what the Bible says about the importance of verbal assent:

Deuteronomy 6:7

Psalm 37:30

Psalm 71:24

Colossians 3:17

Philippians 3:11

Romans 10:9-10

Matthew 28:19-20

Finally, there are many people who argue that because Jesus often discouraged people from telling others about Himself early in His ministry, this means we should also be reticent to talk about God. Why do you think Jesus waited until after His death and resurrection to issue the Great Commission? When answering, think about the shift between "not yet" and "Go ye therefore…."

Do we have to talk? Absolutely. What we say, and how we say it, now becomes the journey.

COMPANION STUDY FOR CHAPTER 3,
"THE ART OF GENTLE PERSUASION"

Breaking Down the Walls Gently

(John 5:4-42)

In this study's companion chapter we lay out a set of assumptions. React to each of them from your own experiences in the workplace:

1. Most of our co-workers have not read the Bible themselves. Any knowledge they have of it has come to them secondhand.

2. Many people who profess to be Christians *also* only have secondhand knowledge of the contents of the Bible. They get it in sermons, from devotions, in Bible stories—but they seldom get it directly from the source. Often these professing Christians with secondhand knowledge of the Bible are the secondhand sources of our co-workers.

3. Even those who actually read the Bible can only understand the Gospel message at first. The "secret decoder ring" for understanding the message of the Bible is a personal relationship with Jesus Christ. With that relationship comes the presence of the Holy Spirit, who moves in our hearts to teach us the full force and effect of all of Scripture. This is an urgent point, because a discussion of the Bible between a follower of Christ and someone who is not *will never be on a level playing field. (This assumption is perhaps the most important point workplace Christians must grasp in talking to their co-workers. Don't debate the peripherals, focus on the matter at hand: your concern for their spiritual condition.)*

4. Generally, our co-workers do not naturally want to talk about matters of faith. They do, however, have a higher degree of tolerance for listening to our story of faith.

5. Almost universally, people at work are interested in talking about themselves. Therein lies the most important tool in the art of gentle persuasion.

Read through the entire passage (John 5:4-42) once. Compare the Samaritan woman's response to Christ to what you know of the response of most of the Pharisees of His day. Why do you think there was such a difference in the responses?

Can you identify people or groups who qualify as "Samaritans" in your workplace? List them.

What about parallels to the Pharisees? List people or groups in your workplace who may parallel the Pharisees of Jesus' days.

Are the "Samaritans" in your workplace more or less likely to hear you discuss your faith at work than the "Pharisees"? Why do you think that may be true?

Of those two groups, which is likely to make dramatic changes as a result of seeing Christ in your life and hearing Him in your testimony? Why do you think that may be true?

Study Jesus' communications with the Samaritan woman from the passage above, the woman caught in adultery, and Zaccheus in the passages below. Describe the evidences of Jesus' gentleness in these encounters.

John 8:2-11

Luke 19:1-10

Now look again at Jesus' conversation with the woman at the well, especially in John 4:16. Why do you think he told her to call her husband?

What impact did His response in verses 17 and 18 have on her, and why?

Does this suggest another step in the process of gently persuading our co-workers to consider Christ? What is it?

How does knowing the details of our co-workers' lives affect our desire to have them know Christ? How does knowing those details enable us to talk about God with them? In what ways does our knowledge of the details of their lives make them more interested in hearing what we have to say about faith?

Now look at verses 10 and 13-14 of John 4. What is Jesus doing with His statements here?

What does that suggest as another step in the process of gently persuading others to consider Christ?

Throughout this passage, we see evidence that Jesus listened closely to the things the woman was saying. Why is that important in a conversation about God? Why is this particularly true for today's workplace?

Finally, describe how Jesus moved the woman from her own questions to the truth about Him. In what ways can we apply that principle in our own discussions?

Gentle persuasion often takes a person from their point of interest to a sense of curiosity and then to a phase of conversation. When the conversation turns into exploration, the real meat of communicating our faith begins.

COMPANION STUDY FOR CHAPTER 4,
"LEARNING THE IMPORTANCE OF SILENCE"

When We Shouldn't Speak

Are there times when we should not talk about God on the job? List examples of times when you think it might not be appropriate to talk about God at work.

In a later study we'll tackle two areas we think are times when silence about our faith is important at work: when it distracts us or our co-workers from the task at hand, and when our co-workers aren't interested. Before leaving them, though, how might trying to evangelize in these two circumstances harm our testimony for Christ?

Think of a time when you've violated either of these premises. What effects did it have on the workplace? On your co-workers?

How would you answer someone who says the fate of a soul is always more important than the task at hand?

Assuming you agree with these first two premises, in what ways do recognizing and abiding by them actually improve your ability to talk about God at other times on the job?

What harm is done when we force our co-workers to listen after they've made it clear they aren't interested?

What should be our proper response to co-workers who are not interested?

Now examine the exchange between Jesus and Caiaphas in Matthew 26:57-64. Remember that those who don't have a personal relationship with Jesus Christ as Savior are not able to understand the mystery of Christ's atonement. With that in mind, why do you think Jesus did not respond to the queries made of Him at His trial?

Were Christ's questioners interested in finding the truth at His trial? What parts of this passage lead you to answer in the way you did? Do you think their motivation played a role in Jesus' decision to be silent? If so, what principle does that suggest for us in trying to determine when to be silent?

Find the passage in Scripture where Jesus uses the phrase "wipe the dust off your feet." What are the parallels between that passage and this encounter with the high priest?

Second, where would the discussions at the trial have ended if Jesus had answered any other questions than the one He finally answered?

What information finally emerged when Jesus did speak? What does this suggest as a reason for remaining silent in stormy debates over moral issues and challenges to our faith?

Our primary objective must always be to move people to a place where they can hear the good news of redemption through Jesus Christ. Often, silence in emotional debates, in the face of ridicule, in the face of insincere questioners, and even in the face of harmless rabbit trails will lead the discussions back to the only point that matters: a declaration that Jesus is the Good News.

COMPANION STUDY FOR CHAPTER 5,
"WHAT MUST BE UNDERSTOOD,
WHAT MUST BE SAID"

Knowing What to Say

Talking about God in today's workplace requires us to communicate clearly in language our co-workers can understand. However, before we can translate the good news of Jesus Christ into words that make sense to others, we must understand the principles clearly ourselves. We must also know the difference between what we understand and what we must say. Not everything we know about our faith can be grasped by someone who lacks the Holy Spirit in his or her life. So, while we must endeavor to understand a great deal about our faith, we must work equally hard to communicate only what can be understood at first.

We must also remember that each person will have a different capacity to learn.

Read 1 Corinthians 2:14-16. Who does this passage say may understand the truths of God? And what equips them to do so?

Who cannot understand these truths? Why?

What does this establish, then, as the primary information to be communicated in our discussions of God?

Find a Bible that offers introductions to each of its books. Take a few minutes and read the introductions to the four Gospels—-Matthew, Mark, Luke and John.

Let's examine Matthew first. In a Bible dictionary, look up Matthew and read all the passages where Matthew is mentioned. (We call this a biblical biography, and it's an excellent way to approach a study of the Scriptures. For example, reading King David's "biography" from Scripture gives us an excellent view of how God is involved in the details of human beings, even when they falter.) Describe Matthew's background, taking special note of his religious and ethnic history.

Notice who Matthew has in mind when he writes. Why would one of the four Gospels be directed toward Jews?

Now do the same exercise with Mark, Luke and John. Exploring these introductions, we discover Matthew, Mark and Luke directed their writings to different ethnic groups. Describe these groups' likely familiarity with the expectation of a Messiah.

John's book communicates the love of Christ intimately. Remembering that John was the "disciple whom Jesus loved," why is this logical?

Recognizing that knowing Christ is the key to understanding the rest of the New Testament—indeed, also to understanding the Old Testament—is it any wonder that four separate accounts of Christ's time on earth are recorded? Notice these four "road maps" converge in Acts, Luke's second part to his tale of the Christ. What does this suggest about the ability of the Gospel message to penetrate all cultures?

Now think of your workplaces. Remembering the groups you described above and how they might view differently the concept of Messiah, identify your co-workers under one of the following four categories:

Matthew: Co-workers familiar with the Bible, or believing themselves to be, but not apparently having a personal relationship with Jesus Christ.

Mark: Co-workers who are successful, have little time or interest in faith and see it as a crutch for the weak. These people are likely to only be interested in the facts, and probably not in other details of the story of Christ.

Luke: Little or no knowledge of Scripture. Everything you tell them, or nearly everything you tell them, is new to them. These people likely form the largest number of people in your workplace, though most of your co-workers might place themselves in the Matthew category. Keep in mind this category may also include people who attend church, but who know little of the Bible's content.

John: These are the co-workers who are struggling and whose lives are waiting for the catharsis of hope, or the dream of change.

Below, complete an outline of the need for Christ, using these four headings. Support each point with Scriptures.

I. God's Desire for Relationship With Us, and Sin's Impact on It

II. People Are Not Basically Good, and Our Inability to Restore Relationship

III. The Exclusivity of Christ

IV. The Work of Christ

V. Our Response

Very rarely will we get the chance at work to whip out a Bible tract and walk someone through an entire Gospel presentation, if for no other reason than time constraints. Very rarely will we get the chance to recount for someone on the job the entire story of what Christ has done in our own lives. This, then, argues for a cumulative telling of the story, built up in tiny bits over many conversations. Yet, it is urgent for us to consciously move them forward through their journey toward faith in a systematic fashion, remembering what we've told them and searching for opportunities to give them more of the total picture. In short, we must concentrate on communicating the central story of Christ above all other aspects of our faith if we are to partner with God in our places of work.

COMPANION STUDY FOR CHAPTER 6,
"READY TO GIVE AN ANSWER"

Showing Ourselves Approved

Always be prepared to give an answer to everyone who asks you to give the reason for the hope that you have. 1 Peter 3:15

Describe in your own words what Peter is saying in this verse, and then relate it to talking about God in the workplace.

Recount below a time when you were asked to give an answer to spiritual questions on the job. Describe the question, and the reason you think it was posed.

Were you able to answer the question to your satisfaction? Were you able to answer the question to *their* satisfaction? (Not that they agreed, but that your answer was consistent or logical.)

What made it possible for you to answer the question, or if unable to do so, what would have enabled you to answer the question?

Explore the following Scripture passages, and describe what they tell us about our need to be prepared:

1 Corinthians 13:1-3

2 Timothy 2:14-15

2 Timothy 3:16-4:5

Psalm 119:11

Psalm 119:105

In the companion chapter to this study, we describe more fully the following five steps we think might help you be prepared to give answers.

1. Examining a statement of faith from your church, write out on a separate sheet of paper your own personal statement of faith. This will likely take longer than a group study will give it, so be prepared for this to be an ongoing exercise. In doing so, attempt to discover why you believe each statement. Being able to give answers to spiritual questions in the marketplace most often means not only giving those answers, but being able to demonstrate why you believe them. We've discovered that as people use Scripture to understand for themselves why their beliefs are true, a wonderful thing happens: they discover the Holy Spirit makes it possible for them to grasp even the complex truths of the Bible.

2. Understand that reading books about the Bible is not the same as reading the Bible. Likewise, reading devotions that describe the truths of Scripture is not the same as reading the Bible itself. Books about the Bible and devotions describing the Bible are excellent helps, but they can never cement the truth of Scripture for you. What is cemented in your heart becomes the answer you are always ready to give.

3. Establish a regular pattern to your Bible studies. In our companion chapter we mention themed studies, but there are many ways to study the Bible. "Spiritual biographies," discussed elsewhere in these studies, offer vivid pictures of how God works in our lives. They encourage us to understand why the events of that person's life occurred and, more importantly, were selected for inclusion in the canon.

4. Explore writers like C. S. Lewis, Francis Schaeffer, James Boice, Martin Lloyd-Jones and other Christians whose handling of Scripture have stood the test of time. This will not only help you understand Scripture but relate what you learn to the culture of the workplace. Apologetics works are not only useful in offering you answers to tough

questions to share with others, but they also answer the tough questions you're asking. These often serve as excellent confidence builders, but again, we caution you to explore the Bible yourself to prove the truth and wisdom of the writings. Reading truth best enables you to appropriate it. Appropriating it in your own life best enables you to share it with someone you work with, or someone you love.

5. Finally, explore the tough questions ahead of time. You know what they are because you ask them yourself. Why is there pain? How can a good God…? Why doesn't God save everybody? Exploring the questions for yourself means you'll be ready for them when you get them to work.

One final note of warning. Avoid showing off your newfound knowledge. Remember from our earlier chapters that people without Christ are not able to fully understand the truths of Scripture. While it's terrific to offer pertinent answers to their questions, we must never forget our objective is to steer them back to the story of Christ. Every answer we give on the tough issues should leave a path to Christ open in its answer. We know of many Christians who can defend their faith admirably, but never guide their listeners past an admiration of their biblical acumen. Knowledge is important, spiritual growth is desirable, but the story of God is about relationship.

Few works make this as clear as the *Billy Graham Workers Handbook*, a tool used to train the phone volunteers who field calls after a televised Billy Graham gathering. In intriguing, pointed and often poignant ways, the book demonstrates vividly the way to answer hard questions while keeping a personal relationship with Jesus Christ at the center of the purpose of the communication. We do well to mimic that book in the faith conversations that take place on the job.

Many other resources exist, including *Christianity Explored*, a work produced by a church in London, and the materials used by Alpha.

COMPANION STUDY FOR CHAPTER 7,
"...NOT FORGETTING TO PRAY"

The Preparation of Prayer

Evangelism is a multi-faceted activity. While we as believers are called to give testimony to what the Lord is doing in our lives (and what He did in His act of grace), those are but acts of faithful gratitude. The Holy Spirit works at two levels in our relationships with our co-workers. First, it's the Holy Spirit who softens their hearts, preparing them to hear the testimonies we offer. Remembering this should encourage us as we realize the supernatural partnership we enter into when we seek to talk about God at work. Second, the Holy Spirit is active in *our* efforts, blessing even our most feeble acts when made with a heart of gratitude and a desire to be faithful

Describe below what you believe to be the purpose of prayer.

What do you think these Scriptures are teaching us about the *importance* of prayer?

Luke 5:16; Luke 9:18; Luke 11:1; Luke 3:21-22; Luke 6:12-16

Luke 18:1

James 1:5

Matthew 6:13

Though the Bible describes many other reasons why prayer is important, we want to stress one more: prayer shifts our focus from ourselves to God. When we pray, we actively acknowledge our submissive relationship to the Father, and this action helps us cement this truth in the rest of our lives. Prayer is our recognition that God is in control, and prayers about our efforts to talk about God at work remind us He's in control of that area as well.

Many Christians have been taught to how to pray using the acronym ACTS. Examine how these four words fit into our prayer lives:

Adoration: Matthew 6:9; Daniel 4:34-35. How do we express our love for God? What are some of the ways we can make this part of our prayers—recognizing the work He's done for us and recognizing His majesty?

Confession: Matthew 6:12; 1 John 1:9. Why is confession important? Can you think of other Scriptures that describe why confession is a necessary part of our relationship with God, and thus a necessary part of our prayers? List those passages here.

Thanksgiving: 1 Thessalonians 5:18; Philippians 4:6. On top of scriptural commands to give thanks, why do you think offering expressions of gratitude might be an important part of our prayer lives?

Supplication: 1 Timothy 2:1-3; Matthew 6:11; and 6:13. In this part of our prayers, we make our requests known to Him. Why (and how) would the first three affect the last one?

Think of the people you meet in your jobs. What are some of the ways you might prepare yourself during your prayer times to talk to them about God?

What might be the value of the following ideas?
Praying over your calendar for the day:

Praying for those you lead or manage:

Praying for those who lead or manage you: (Can you think of a Scripture passage that points to this obligation? If so, list it here.)

Asking God to show us who we should speak to about Him:

The work of evangelism is the work of the Holy Spirit. The work of evangelism is our work. As the Holy Spirit softens hearts, including our own, so too does prayer change the way we see those who need to hear about salvation.

COMPANION STUDY FOR CHAPTER 8,
"RESPONSIBLE WORKERS"

Responsible Workplace Evangelism

American Christians talk a lot about the restrictions their companies place on their religious activities. In most instances, though, the prohibitions have more to do with the way we talk about God, and not the content. To be blunt, our problem is less about legal or corporate restrictions and more about the offensive ways some Christians bring God up at work. While that statement is likely to rankle some, it needs to be explored in any serious discussion of evangelism on the job.

This smokescreen against evangelism may make us feel comfortable, but it's a paper barrier. The real conversations around workplace faith discussions should be centered on correcting our behavior rather than emphasizing the legal prohibitions. Harm is done to the Kingdom when we shirk our responsibilities as employees, especially when evangelism is the reason we do so.

Think of your workplace. What are the barriers to talking about God at your job? Include in your list what you believe are the legal barriers, what are company policy barriers, what are physical barriers (e.g., you don't work near anyone), and what are the intangible barriers, like your fear of rejection.

Many Christians are surprised to discover that talking about God at work, when it isn't disruptive to the flow of work, can actually be *legally protected*. The most important ingredient in this legal protection, though, is establishing that you sincerely believe God commands you to do so.

In what ways do the following verses equip you to do that?

Matthew 10:32

Matthew 28:19-20

Deuteronomy 6:6-9

1 Peter 3:15

Why might it be especially difficult for managers to talk to their subordinates about their faith?

One of the barriers to effective work/faith integration is the incorrect notion that faith is a private matter and shouldn't affect our work. This dichotomy is not consistent with Scripture. Often when working believers are coached in sharing their faith on the job, they're told to do so only during breaks. Given the need to eliminate the dichotomy of work and faith in separate worlds, why would this advice be inappropriate?

Christians have an obligation to consider carefully how their words and actions on the job reflect on God. This means every aspect of their work must be taken into account as we fulfill the role Paul reminds us we have as ambassadors for Christ (2 Corinthians 5:20).

What are some of the common errors Christians make on the job?

In Matthew 17:24-27, Jesus outwits Pharisees who were trying to trap him into offending the Roman Empire. What principle in this passage instructs us about our responsibility to our employers?

Describe times when you've either violated that principle or seen others violate it. What are some of the possible effects of doing so?

Discuss the following statements in light of their impact on conversations about God at work:

Christians often use words to represent Christ when their actions have not earned them a measure of respect. (See Colossians 3:23)

Words of faith are often shrill when expressed outside of relationship.

Christians often emphasize the negatives in their discussions about God.

Christians often criticize other Christians in front of their co-workers.

Our knowledge of Scripture is poor.

Our witness to the goodness of God and the effects of Christ on our lives is easily diminished by careless approaches to integrity, competency and sensitivity. We must be "wise as serpents, but gentle as doves" as we serve on the front lines of His work in our workplaces.

COMPANION STUDY FOR CHAPTER 9,
"COME, LET US REASON TOGETHER"

Scripture Is Truth

While a non-Christian may be unwilling to accept Scripture as absolute truth, or to understand the bulk of its teachings, it does not mean we cannot express our faith in logical terms that appeal to a person's intellect. In fact, Christians have often been far too willing to abandon a commitment to the truth of Scripture, to abandon our ability to reasonably explain why our faith is consistent with God's creation, to abandon efforts to describe why our worldview—a Christian worldview—is the only one that makes sense. That willingness to surrender truth and reason to scoffers and humanists only makes it more difficult for thinking people to consider Christ, and, worse, makes it more difficult for the next generation to believe in Jesus Christ.

Our tendency to describe what we do as a leap of faith suggests there is no logic to it. It further suggests we must suspend our rational selves in order to participate in the spiritual.

Read Acts 17:16-32.

Remembering our discussion of the four Gospels and their targets, which of the four Gospels would likely have been targeted to the Athenians? Why do you think that's true?

Describe what you think the Apostle Paul was doing in this passage.

Examine Acts 17:16 in relation to verse 23 of the same chapter. What has Paul done here?

What emerges as a principle as we seek to discuss our faith in the marketplace? Why do stormy debates rarely produce converts?

List below the progression Paul made intellectually from his observations on the unknown God to the place where he declares the Resurrection.

Why would this have been important to the Athenians?

Now read Luke 1:1-4. Again, remembering his audience, what does Luke hope to do with his record in the books of Luke and Acts?

Now read Paul's defense before Felix in Acts 24, before Festus in Acts 25, and again before Agrippa in Acts 26.

These are extraordinary examples of Paul's understanding that we do not have to disengage our brains in order to believe in God. Why is that helpful in talking about God in today's workplace?

Our culture today dismisses the Bible as absolute truth. In fact, many in our culture argue there are no absolute truths. What do the following Scriptures say about this issue?

Psalms 119:142-160

John 14:6

John 14:17

John 17:17, 19

Galatians 2:5,14

The following passages argue for our integration of truth into our lives. Discuss how these verses support that integration:

Ephesians 4:29

3 John 3, 4

John 4:23-24

1 Timothy 4:3

2 Timothy 2:15

1 Peter 1:22

2 Peter 1:12

So, what does this mean for the marketplace Christian?

It means we must make our faith a part of our entire being, exploring it intellectually as we experience it in our relationship with God. The hard questions we fail to answer for ourselves are the hard questions our co-workers often want to ask us, and our inability to address them makes our God seem like fantasy, not the reality we know Him to be.

It means we must confront the doubts we have about the accuracy of Scripture head-on, studying it closely to see how it overcomes the false charges of inconsistency, contradiction and inaccuracy. Rather than being afraid of what such a journey might uncover, our confidence in God as the author of truth should cause us to set out on that journey in boldness.

Such a journey also provides us with terrific discussion material at work. The deep issues of life are universal questions, and our ability to speak authoritatively on them to career-minded co-workers who consider themselves enlightened is a powerful icebreaker on the path to telling them about Christ.

COMPANION STUDY FOR CHAPTER 10,
"WHAT IF THEY SAY YES?!"

Steps of Discipleship

"If any man be in Christ, he is a new creature: old things are passed away; behold, all things are become new." 2 Corinthians 5:17

"Sirs, what must I do to be saved?"

How very rare those words are in our culture today. Yet, rare as they are, they point to the certainty that God does indeed draw to Himself people in our circles of influence. When that occurs, when a person responds to Christ and looks to us for guidance in the next steps of the journey of faith, what should we do?

First, we must understand the urgent importance of fellowship and community at that point in their spiritual journey. Particularly in the case of the workplace, someone who comes to know Christ as their Savior is likely to experience changes that will affect their work relationships. Some will lose friends because of those changes; others may even need to change jobs. This sudden earthquake in their spiritual world is paralleled by its impact on their physical world. Hit and run evangelism, which moves on to the next "victim" once we "slide another soul inside the pearly gates" often leaves the new believer bewildered and uncomfortable. Immediately following conversion, we need to move alongside them to help them understand the changes they are experiencing.

We also need to help them find a church, where they can begin to understand the importance of the Body of Christ in their spiritual growth. Even when we're able to spend large blocks of time with a young believer, the blessings of being in a community of believers are immeasurable. Just seeing and knowing other intelligent people embrace faith is an encouragement.

For those whom God places in our path, we share a responsibility not only to tell them about Christ, but also to help them in their spiritual journey after they receive Him. This is commonly referred to as discipleship. But how do we help them grow? What goals should we be working toward as we help them understand this life of faith?

Examine Matthew 28:19-20. While we often term this the Great Commission and use it as a basis for imploring for evangelism, discuss the discipleship component in this passage.

Jesus' relationship with His own disciples offers us some clues about what we should be trying to do with those who are given to us by the Holy Spirit to disciple. Identify some of the aspects of discipleship seen in these passages:

Luke 6:20-38

Luke 11:1

Luke 12:22

Luke 24:36-43

Luke 24:44-45

Now prepare your own discipleship template. In our companion chapter we list five items from a longer list by a missionary author to serve as a pattern for discipling a new believer. Using your own knowledge of Scripture, and a concordance and Bible dictionary, support each of the following with passages from the Bible.

After establishing a new believer in a community of believers, we should train them to experience:

1. *A life yielded to God and controlled by His Spirit.* (Search for the role of the Holy Spirit in your Bible dictionaries.)

2. *A restful trust in God for the supply of all needs.* (Search for passages about depending on God for this section.)

3. *A sympathetic spirit and a willingness to take a lowly place.* (Search for passages on humility and compassion for this section.)

4. *Love for communion with God and for the study of His Word.* (Re-explore some of the earlier lessons in this study for any passages that illustrate the need for prayer and Bible study.) Remember ACTS?

Adoration: Matthew 6:9; Daniel 4:34-35

Confession: Matthew 6:12; 1 John 1:9

Thanksgiving: 1 Thessalonians 5:18; Philippians 4:6

Supplication: 1 Timothy 2:1-3; Matthew 6:11,13

5. *Some experience and blessing in the Lord's work at home, the local church.* In order to be strong in the culture where we work, we must draw on the strength of the Body of Christ. While equipping ourselves and others for faith initiatives in our jobs, we should never overlook the importance of connecting new believers to a local church.

Fellowship. Commitment to absolute truth. Humility. Prayer. Confidence in God's provision. These form solid ground for young believers to begin their own exploration of faith.

Resources from Marketplace Network

One of the most frustrating struggles marketplace Christians face as they try to apply their faith to work is locating relevant and reliable resources. Since 1993 Marketplace Network has been creating written and audio materials to meet this demand, as well as pointing the way to works by other marketplace organizations, giving you valuable insights from a wide range of writers and speakers. Here are just some of the resources available from our catalog and web site.

30 Moments Christians Face in the Workplace
3-Volume Study Series

What tough issues do YOU face in your workplace? And how do you go about applying your faith to your work? To help you on this journey, Marketplace Network's Randy Kilgore has written a challenging series of small group studies based on what we call the "30 Moments of Truth." These "30 Moments" make up our *"Work As Ministry" Framework* — a theological framework for understanding our work and the marketplace. It provides a way of understanding and resolving many of the toughest issues we face in the workplace, as well as a path to changing ourselves into the kind of ambassadors for Christ that are reflected throughout the Bible.

Each Study Guide covers 10 of the "30 Moments" — in the context of the Great Commandment (Volume I), the Great Commission (Volume II) and the Cultural Mandate (Volume III). Each Study Guide also contains an in-depth introduction to the *"Work As Ministry" Framework*. Leader Guides are available for each volume to assist small group leaders in facilitating discussion and in getting the most out of each lesson.

Marketplace Forum Audiotapes

Marketplace Network hosts bi-monthly breakfasts in the greater Boston area featuring seasoned business and professional leaders who share some of their own experiences about the benefits of applying their faith to their work. These events are held in traditional business settings and are geared to business executives, marketplace workers, pastors and church members who wish to learn while enjoying the fellowship of others with common interests and struggles. Audiotapes are available of each forum, and many have been packaged into groups of six tapes centered on a common theme. Speakers include: **John Beckett, Russ Crosson, Chuck Colson, Mary Ann Glendon, Os Guiness, Ray Hammond, Timothy Johnson, Andrew Mills, Haddon Robinson,** and others.

Marketplace Ministry Starter Kit

Recognizing that the church plays a key role in ministering to and discipling marketplace Christians, we have designed a kit which includes many of the tools necessary for a church to start its own marketplace ministry.

CALL 617-227-4226 TO ORDER A CATALOG, OR VISIT OUR WEB SITE:
www.marketplace-network.org